D1488420

GENDER THREAT

American Masculinity in the Face of Change

Dan Cassino and Yasemin Besen-Cassino

STANFORD UNIVERSITY PRESS
Stanford, California

Stanford University Press
Stanford, California

Printed in the United States of America on acid-free, archival-quality paper

Library of Congress Cataloging-in-Publication Data

Names: Cassino, Dan, 1980- author. | Besen-Cassino, Yasemin, author.
Title: Gender threat : American masculinity in the face of change / Dan Cassino and Yasemin Besen-Cassino.
Description: Stanford, California : Stanford University Press, 2021. | Includes bibliographical references and index.
Identifiers: LCCN 2021018468 (print) | LCCN 2021018469 (ebook) | ISBN 9781503610361 (cloth) | ISBN 9781503629899 (paperback) |
ISBN 9781503629905 (epub)
Subjects: LCSH: Masculinity—United States. | Men—United States—Identity. | Gender identity—United States.
Classification: LCC HQ1090.3 .C385 2021 (print) | LCC HQ1090.3 (ebook) | DDC 305.310973—dc23
LC record available at https://lccn.loc.gov/2021018468
LC ebook record available at https://lccn.loc.gov/2021018469

Cover design: Michel Vrana

Cover photo: iStock

Typeset by Newgen North America in 10/14 Mercury Text G1

CONTENTS

ACKNOWLEDGMENTS

We were invited to the University Gothenburg during the summer of 2018. The Gender Diversity Workshop held there in June 2018 was essential for the theoretical conceptualization of our book. We would like to thank Aliya Saperstein, Laurel Westbrook, Katie Bolzendahl, Lena Wängnerud, Elizabeth Goodyear-Grant, Amanda Bittner, and Johanna Rickne.

We are also grateful to the teams at Data For Progress, CIDE Mexico, and our colleagues at the FDU/PublicMind Poll for providing essential data.

We would like to thank the wonderful team at Stanford University Press, especially our editor Marcela Cristina Maxfield. We also thank our series editors Paula England and David Grusky for their insightful comments and suggestions.

We would like to acknowledge a Career Development Grant from Montclair State University. And we thank our graduate assistant Hean Zeidner Kaspi, who helped us to code blogs and websites for our discussion in Chapter 6.

GENDER THREAT

CHAPTER 1

THREATENED IDENTITY

Against all evidence, American men have come to believe that the world—economically, socially, politically—is tilted against them. Sure, 95 percent of Fortune 500 CEOs are men, along with more than 80 percent of members of Congress, men still earn significantly more money than women for the same work, and men have an unbeaten 45 and 0 record of winning the American Presidency, but even so, the 2012 American National Election Study found that 41 percent of Republican men say they face at least a "moderate amount of discrimination" because of their gender. Even among men identifying as Democrats, a majority say that they face at least "a little bit" of sex discrimination. Believing that men are somehow disadvantaged in today's society may seem silly, but those beliefs are based in something very real: the tension between how men view their own roles at home, at work, and in society, and the reality of a society in which their privilege is being reduced. Men still enjoy a lot of advantages in our society, but those advantages—especially for white men in working-class jobs—are not as great as they used to be. When you've been on top for a few thousand years, even small moves toward equality can feel like discrimination.

But the key to understanding men's sense of losing ground isn't the movement toward equality. The key is the beliefs that men hold, their own ideas of what being a man means. We refer to this as a man's *gender identity,* which consists of that man's beliefs about the behaviors and attitudes that make him a man. This gender identity is entirely separate from a person's sex, which, while more complicated than most people think of it as being, is closer to being a biological characteristic.

As we'll show, the conceptions men have of their own gender are both flexible and remarkably fragile. They're flexible in that—under the right circumstances—men are able to abandon an aspect of their gender identity that isn't working, and replace it with one that is without too much difficulty. For instance, we came across men who found they were no longer the chief earners in their households, but who compensated by buying a gun, or going to church, or spending more time with their kids.

And men's gender identity is fragile in that masculinity is earned, in many societies through trials or rituals, and can be lost if a man fails to live up to the demands of his gender. As West and Zimmerman (1987) put it, men "do gender," and perform masculinity in their everyday lives. There are many reasons why someone might not feel like or be perceived as "a real man." Men put up a performance of gender—as detailed in the work of Judith Butler (1988)—of manhood: they do what Michael Schwalbe (2005) refers to as "manhood acts." At times, however, maybe they feel they're not supporting their family, or living up to a moral or behavioral code, or standing up for themselves, or maybe they feel they're physically or emotionally weak. Such perceptions can threaten men's gender identities, so men must be vigilant about monitoring threats to their gender identity and bolstering it as needed, finding ways to assert their masculinity in the face of the threat. While there is a societally transmitted set of behaviors and attitudes commonly associated with masculinity—what R. W. Connell (1987) has termed *hegemonic masculinity*—the components of individual men's gender identities do vary widely, as do their responses to failures to live up to their own standards of masculinity. When failing to fulfill the ideals of hegemonic masculinity, many men resort to what sociologists refer to as "compensatory manhood acts" (Sumerau 2012). These compensatory acts, as we'll illustrate, can take many forms, but they all serve the same end: the bolstering of an endangered gender identity.

In addition to sociologists, psychologists—most notably the early Freudian Alfred Adler (2002)—have thought of this endangered identity as a deep, existential threat to men. While we're not Freudians, there is ample evidence that men engage in all sorts of otherwise inexplicable behaviors in order to compensate for threats to their gender identity. This book shines a light on the sorts of things that men perceive as threats, or potential threats, to their masculine gender identities, and then shows how men adjust their behaviors and attitudes to compensate for those threats.

Understanding this perceived threat has become more urgent in recent years, as gender issues have become a larger part of our social and political discourse. In recent years, Americans have seen misogyny fueled mass shootings (Issa 2019), a US President who seems unconcerned with the use of what he calls "locker room talk," public handwringing over the transition from male-dominated manufacturing and extractive industries to a service economy, the revelation of rampant sexual harassment in workplaces and among high-powered figures in the media, and so much more. Why is all of this happening now? A lot of what people are experiencing is fallout from the Great Recession of 2008 and 2009.

THE GREAT RECESSION

The US economy has experienced many recessions previously, but the recession that started in 2008 with the mortgage bust was unique in its disproportionate impact on men. This impact led Mark Perry, a professor of economics at the University of Michigan-Flint, to refer to it as a "mancession" in his testimony before Congress in 2010 (Perry 2010), a description that has filtered down to the public understanding of the crisis.

The 2008 and 2009 recession officially lasted nearly two years, from December 2007 through June 2009, and at least in its initial stages, affected mostly men. According to the Brookings Institution's Hamilton Project (Swanson 2017), 70 percent of the jobs lost during the recession were held by men. This more than doubled men's unemployment rates, which rapidly went from 4 percent to about 11 percent. According to 2014 figures from the Economic Policy Institute, more than 6 million men lost their jobs, compared to just 2.7 million women, between the end of 2007 and the end of 2009 (Wething 2014).

Economists Hillary Hoynes, Douglas Miller, and Jessamyn Schaller (2012), using population surveys and national time series data, found that the effects of the Great Recession not only impacted men more than women but also lasted longer for men. Their analysis blames this difference on occupational segregation: men are more likely to be employed in the more cyclical industries such as construction, manufacturing, and financial services: the industries hardest hit by the recession. Women tend to be more concentrated in service industries and the public sector, areas of the economy that weren't hit nearly as hard, at least initially.

In addition to experiencing higher levels of unemployment, men found that their unemployment during the recession lasted longer than that of women. According to the Bureau of Labor Statistics (2019), men between 20 and 44 years of age who lost their jobs during the recession stayed jobless for an average of 26 to 33 weeks, much longer than the average unemployed woman at that time. Even that figure of 6 to 8 months of unemployment—on average!—understates the length of time it took men to get back to work, as official "unemployment" measures cut off either when someone gets a job or gets so discouraged by their failure to get a job that they stop looking. It's no surprise that this period coincided with a spike in Social Security disability claims, as some men decided that getting benefits was a more likely scenario than finding a job. In February 2009, the labor force participation rate (the proportion of Americans 16 and older who have, or are looking for, a job, a figure that includes the "discouraged" workers not counted in the unemployment figures) was 65.8 percent. By 2019, the recession had been over for almost 10 years, but the labor force participation rate hasn't gone above 63.2 percent. Between 2006 and 2016, men's labor force participation rates dropped by 4 points, from 74 percent to 70 percent. Women's participation dropped as well, but by only 2 points, from 59 to 57 percent. Some of that shift is driven by an aging population, but much of it comes from people just giving up on work: while the labor force participation rate had been declining for some time before the Great Recession, the recession led to a dramatic acceleration of that shift.

Of course, not all men were equally affected by the recession. Race and ethnicity played an important role in access to jobs. By the end of the recession, in 2009, African-American men had the highest unemployment rate, followed by Latino men (18% and 13.9%, respectively). Between 2008 and 2010, white (and separately, Asian) men's unemployment increased by about 3.5 points; among African-American men, the increase was 5.9 points, and among Latino men, it was 4.9 points. Younger and less educated men were also impacted more (Adjeiwaa-Manu 2017).

While the early part of the recession was disproportionately felt by men, the reaction to the recession was disproportionately felt by women. As state and local governments faced revenue shortfalls because of the increased need for services and decreased tax revenue, many engaged in austerity programs. These cuts—laying off teachers and other public sector workers—led to increased unemployment among women, even as the labor market for men started to recover.

While the recession officially ended in 2009, the effects on the labor market lasted much longer, with men in particular seeing effects long afterward. According to the Brookings Institution, the total number of jobs in the United States reached pre-recession levels in April of 2014. But while jobs have returned, they have not come back in the same industries where they were lost. Manufacturing, construction, and extractive industries—all of which are among the most disproportionately male sectors of the economy—have all been slow to recover. This has made the recovery from the recession uneven for men (Schanzenbach et al. 2017), as sectors that employ them haven't shown the robust gains of other parts of the economy.

As the shifts in the labor force participation rates show, the recession was a jolt to the economic system, but it mostly served to accelerate trends already in place. As economist Alan Krueger (2016) finds, the labor force participation rates of men 25 to 54 years old have been trending downward for the past few decades. The manufacturing jobs that were lost in the recession were already on their way out, as labor-intensive processes have moved overseas, and automation has reduced the need for human labor. But the recession concentrated a decade or more of these trends into a year or two. The immediacy and shock of this rapid change may also have contributed to the effects of the recession, making them felt in ways that would have been less noticeable or mitigated entirely if the economy had arrived at the same place more gradually.

We talk a lot about unemployment because the US government is very good at collecting and promulgating unemployment figures, broken down by any demographic you might care to think of. But unemployment is just one of the ways in which the shock of the recession has hurt Americans, and American men disproportionately. Hidden in the unemployment figures is the problem of under-employment, in which workers may still have a job, but have fewer hours than they would like, are getting lower pay, or have been forced to switch to part-time or mandatory furloughs or to unpaid leave (Pew Research Center 2010). Workers may also have found new jobs but at greatly reduced pay, or without the benefits or prestige they previously had. They are counted as employed, but they're still feeling the consequences of the recession.

The recession also had an enormous economic impact outside of the loss of jobs or income, in the form of fluctuating home prices. Middle-class Americans have long considered home ownership to be a safe way to build wealth, a view encouraged by government programs that make mortgages more easily available and encourage banks to give out home loans. When home prices started to rise, many Americans saw their wealth, at least on paper, rise alongside them, only to drop dramatically with the mortgage crisis.

In a national 2019 Bankrate survey, 48 percent of Americans said the value of their homes declined during the recession, and 21 percent—10 years after the recession—said they were "underwater," meaning they owed more money than the current market value of their house (Foster 2019). Even if these losses were never realized—few people are willing or able to sell their house for a loss, and may decide instead to wait until prices recover—they still caused Americans to *feel* as though they had lost money. These figures don't include the millions of Americans who engaged in real estate speculation during the boom, and lost big in the bust. The mortgage crisis and its fallout has meant that even many of those Americans who kept their jobs through the recession wound up feeling the pain from it. The impact on the housing market may have been especially jarring for men: providing safe housing is part of the *package deal* (Townsend 2002) of modern US middle-class masculinity.

This increase in economic and financial uncertainty seems to have hit men hard. As part of the American Psychological Association's Mind/Body Health Campaign, a 2009 Harris Interactive poll asked respondents a series of questions about their psychological and emotional health. Harris had asked these questions many times before, but 2009 was the first time that the poll found men more worried than women about finances and their financial future. These worries about money contributed to increased stress overall among men: women's stress levels went up too, but the biggest increases were among men (American Psychological Association 2009).

To some extent, these results merely reflect men catching up to the stress and financial worries that American women have felt for decades, but there's more to them than that. It's one thing for men to lose their jobs, or earn less, or move to a less prestigious position. But these same changes are psychologically more difficult for men when the women around them aren't losing their jobs: when men go from being the breadwinner in the family to making less than their wives, and when men believe they should be able to earn enough to support their families and are angry and ashamed that they can no longer do so. The loss of income is stressful and difficult, especially in a society where so few have savings to tide them over. But the loss of *relative* income, going from earning more than a partner to earning less, may be psychologically more difficult for men, as it requires them to re-think the way they relate to their spouses, their families, and the world.

THE END OF MEN

The Great Recession, and the trends it accelerated, put many men in a declining economic and social position. At the same time, women were gaining ground economically and societally, and as men's positions stalled by some measures, women moved closer to equality. Men are still more likely than women to be in the labor market, but women are catching up. Women are the primary breadwinners in 42 percent of families with children under the age 18, and in another 22 percent of families, they are co-breadwinners (Glynn 2016).

In workplaces, women have been increasingly able to push back against sexist policies or harassment that would have gone unchallenged in decades past. While nothing like all the men who engage in actionable behavior face consequences for doing so, the fact that the possibility of consequences now exists is a huge step forward.

Women have also made substantial gains in education. More than half of the bachelor's degrees awarded today (57 percent) go to women, along with most of the master's degrees (59 percent), and a little over half of the doctoral degrees (52 percent), according to 2018 Catalyst data. Hanna Rosin, in *The End of Men*, notes that this is a stark reversal from earlier periods in the United States, as young men are now much more likely than young women to have only a high school diploma. Research on primary education now openly talks about the "problem with boys," as they fall behind their female classmates at even the earliest levels of education. Colleges have instituted what amounts to affirmative action programs to bring in more male students, as gender-blind admissions policies would lead to overwhelmingly female campuses (Rosin 2012).

None of this is to say that women have achieved social or occupational equality. Even accounting for differences in human capital and occupational areas, the pay gap between men and women remains at somewhere between 10 and 20 cents on the dollar, depending on which controls are included (Blau and Kahn 2017). Women may make up the majority of PhD graduates, but they're still a minority among professors, especially at the higher ranks. They're less likely to be in managerial positions, and are less represented in the science and engineering sectors. There's still talk of women who find themselves confronting a "glass cliff," a scenario in which a woman is promoted to a high-powered position only after a crisis has made that position untenable. Women's reproductive rights have come under renewed attack in some parts of the United States. Women are more than half of the population, but they don't hold anything like half of the seats in the US Congress, nor has a woman ever held the US Presidency.

But despite these continuing inequalities, it's been argued that women will come to dominate society. Rosin (2012) argues that the educational and economic gains of women represent the first steps in what she calls "the end of men." Men's biological advantages, in terms of greater average upper body strength or physical size may have made them more valuable to a society that needed fields plowed, or metal hammered, but, she argues, such traits are less relevant today. There's no reason to believe that men are better suited than women to an information-based economy, and perhaps some reason to believe that women may be more valuable workers.

And indeed, despite existing inequalities, women's progress on all fronts has received extensive coverage, and oftentimes is portrayed as a zero-sum game, with men necessarily losing out. As noted before, moving from a position of dominance toward equality feels a lot like discrimination to the people who used to be on top, and the long-term trends of the increasing status of women and the transitions in the economy have left a lot of men feeling as though they're being marginalized. In the United States, men are seeing their political and social dominance being actively challenged, and as we'll discuss, they find they need to change their gender identities in order to keep up.

"NOT ALL MEN!"

This book spends a lot of time talking about "men," but men are, of course, not a monolithic group. Most of the data we present here derive from sources that don't differentiate on the basis of sexuality, so while it's entirely possible that gay and bisexual men (or those from other sexual orientation and gender identity minority groups) relate to their masculinity in different ways than heterosexual men do, the data to parse those differences out are not available. However, given the research that has been done in this area, and even though gay and bisexual men would define their masculinity differently than heterosexual men do, the likelihood is that the compensation mechanisms we talk about in this book would work in much the same way for both groups (Schilt 2006).

The same caveat can be made for non-white men. While most of our data sources do differentiate on the basis of racial or ethnic group, and we control for these differences when we can, any individual, non-white ethnic group is too small a sample to allow for meaningful analyses. That is, splitting the non-white group apart by ethnicity results in sample sizes that are too small; treating it as a single group ignores enormous differences between ethnic groups. There are surely fascinating and important differences in how men from different racial and ethnic groups construct and defend their masculinities, but looking at those differences is well beyond the scope of this study.

While there are certainly similarities across groups in the way masculinity is defined, every group, and every individual, is going to define masculinity in a different way, and react differently when that definition is threatened. The fact that you, or your husband, or your brother, don't react in the ways described here doesn't mean that the analysis is invalid. It's just that as social scientists, we deal in generalities: how men tend to react, rather than what any particular individual does. Looking at differences between groups can be useful, but we expect that any differences between groups are dwarfed by the enormous variation within any group.

MASCULINITY THEORY

We have already talked a lot about men's gender identities, or masculinities; what might in the past have been called their "gender role." A gender identity is the set of attitudes and behaviors through which a person defines their gender. Men and women alike have gender identities, though women's gender identities tend to be less fragile than those of men. There is a societally agreed upon set of attitudes and behaviors that are considered masculine: the hegemonic masculinity referred to earlier (Connell 1987). These hegemonic masculinities are socially constructed and change according to time and place. Men might deviate from or rebel against them, but even these rebellions necessarily acknowledge how ingrained the ideals of hegemonic masculinity are.

Gender, in this view, isn't something you are, or something you have, but something you do (West and Zimmerman 1987). Individuals create their gender identities through their actions, as a display to those around them, and perhaps most importantly, to themselves. When individuals do something that's at odds with their conception of their gender identity, they feel pressure to make up for it in some way. For instance, in an experiment carried out by psychologists Jennifer Bosson, Jennifer Prewitt-Freilino, and Jenel Taylor (2005), men were brought into the lab, and told that they were part of a study on how well they could learn novel activities. All the men were taught the same task, involving tying strings, but what they didn't know was that they had been randomly assigned to have to have the task described to them as "rope reinforcing" or "hairstyling." All the men were doing the same thing, but while learning rope reinforcing is a perfectly acceptable masculine task, learning how to braid hair is not. Thus, the men who had been braiding hair experienced a threat to their masculine gender identities and felt they had to do something to compensate: in this study, some of them were asked to state aloud some information about themselves. The men who had been told it was a hairstyling task were much more uncomfortable afterward compared to the men doing the rope reinforcing task, and became much more likely to publicly announce their heterosexuality, as opposed to other information that they could have offered. After doing so, those men reported much less discomfort. The men had done something that went against their ideas of what men should do—gay men in the study apparently had no discomfort with the hair braiding description of the task—and had to resolve that feeling. The men who were given the opportunity to announce that, despite braiding hair, they weren't gay, resolved the discomfort. Those who didn't get that opportunity remained uncomfortable.

In the world outside a laboratory, the actions men take to assert their masculine gender identities may be much less sanguine. Connell (1987) has argued that the behaviors embedded in hegemonic masculinities necessarily result in the domination or subordination of women, and at the very least, serve to reinforce existing inequalities.

In his 2002 book *The Package Deal: Marriage, Work and Fatherhood in Men's Lives*, anthropologist Nicholas Townsend (2002) defines modern American masculinity as having four pillars: fatherhood, marriage, homeownership, and employment. These elements are interconnected, and together they comprise what he calls "the package deal." For instance, employment and providing for the family are closely intertwined with being a good father and making sure the children are in a good school district, a safe environment, and a single-family home. In this view, which Townsend holds to be dominant in American society, you simply can't be a good father if you don't have a job or aren't married; just so, you can't be a good husband if you can't have children or don't own a home. These ideals, however, are subject to material constraints, and the pressure to uphold them in an evolving society subjects men to a great deal of stress. Just like the men in the hairstyling study, men who can't meet these standards feel they have to do something to assert their masculine identities. We refer to this state as a gender threat. When in this state, men believe they are falling short of the ideals of masculinity, and they feel pressure to do something about it, to prove that they really are men.

R. W. Connell and James Messerschmidt (2005) have argued that men cope with such threats through the construction of alternative masculinities. Essentially, men have a limited set of societally acceptable ways to express their gender identity, and when circumstances make it difficult or impossible for men to express their gender identity in the way to which they're accustomed, they often look for some other behavior or attitude they can use to bolster the threatened gender identity. Sometimes, these behaviors are beneficial—putting a greater emphasis on fatherhood, for instance. At other times, they can be societally maladaptive: among the behaviors documented in this book are increases in sexual harassment episodes at work, increased opposition to female candidates for public office, increased gun ownership, and a decrease in the amount of time spent on household labor tasks. These behaviors are intended to reinforce men's gender identities, so we refer to them as *compensatory behaviors*, as they're compensating for some gender threat. By engaging in them, men can resolve the pressure caused by the gender threat, and once again be comfortable with their gender identity.

It's important to understand that masculinity is not necessarily the same thing as sexism (though some scholars will argue otherwise). Sexism, as we'll discuss in later chapters, comes in various forms, and while strong masculine identities often go along with sexist views, we take the view that it is possible to express a masculine identity in a way that doesn't involve the denigration of women or femininity. Sexism may be a common result of gender threat, but it isn't a necessary one, especially as more men embrace alternatives to hegemonic masculinity.

These issues of masculinity and how men resolve threats to it have become more pressing in recent years. While men are still dominant in most areas of American society, there is increasing movement toward gender equality; but research on this movement has so far failed to fully explore men's backlash against it. This book focuses on the social, political, and personal effects of the decline in male privilege since the Great Recession of 2008 and 2009. What happens to men's social and political views when they lose their jobs or their status as breadwinners? When a feminist runs for the presidency? When women become more ascendant in the local economy? How do men respond to such threats to their masculine identity?

METHODS

In writing this book, we used a combination of quantitative and qualitative methodologies. On one hand, we're looking at broad social trends, and how threats to men's gender identities are shaping American politics and society. For these sorts of issues, survey data, which can tell us a great deal about *what* is happening, are our best source. For other issues, we're less concerned with what is happening than with *why* it's happening. While we sometimes examine causality by looking at analyses over time, the best way to get at causality is through experiments. If we randomly assign individuals to two groups, treat the groups differently in just one small way, and observe a difference afterward, we can be pretty sure that it was the difference in treatment that led to the different outcomes.

On the other hand, we also make use of qualitative techniques. Knowing what's happening, and why, is useful, but we also sometimes want to know *how* the behaviors we're seeing impact individual men and their families. To find that out, there's no better source than men and their families, and we use content analyses of their stories to get a handle on the lived experience of gender threat.

We use a variety of sources for quantitative data, often using factors like time to link together disparate data sets in order to uncover any connections between them. Foremost among these sources are the General Social Survey, the American National Election Studies, the 2018 AP VoteCast, and economic data from the Bureau of Labor Statistics of the US Department of Labor. We also make use of survey experiments carried out by one of the authors through nationally representative telephone polls, as well as experiments run by others, such as Data For Progress and the

Associated Press. These data sources are supplemented with panel data from sources such as the Pew Research Center and the Cooperative Congressional Election Study, which allow us to track individual men as their attitudes and circumstances change over time, and data from sources such as the US Equal Employment Opportunity Commission, the Federal Bureau of Investigation's firearms background check database, and Google Trends data.

Much of the data is analyzed using time series techniques. A time series approach strengthens an analysis in two ways. First, it allows us to bring together data sets that might not be ordinarily compared: for instance, to look at whether a relationship exists between sexual harassment allegations in a state and the dynamics of gendered unemployment in that state. Data sets that include all the factors we are interested in do not presently exist. Time series analysis allows us to build the data sets we need in order to fully understand the topics we're interested in. Second, the time series approach allows us to make stronger causal claims than can be made from most analyses based on cross-sectional data. The fact that *x* happens before *y* doesn't necessarily mean that *x* is causing *y* (resulting in what researchers call *Granger causality*), but it makes it very difficult to argue that *y* is causing *x*.

We also make use of whatever panel data are available, which also helps us establish causation. While most surveys track changes by looking at different samples of the same population to make inferences about how the population has changed, panel data look at the same individuals over time. Such data sets are rare—mostly because they're much more expensive to produce than data sets from cross-sectional surveys—but they're extremely useful. For instance, men might have more traditional views of the economic role of women because they themselves have lost income, or they may have lost income because of these traditional beliefs. With cross-sectional data, it can be difficult or impossible to sort out what comes first. In a panel, though, we can look at the same individual over time, and show whether changes in one variable came before changes in the other. This doesn't fully solve the issue of causation, of course, but it can help to exclude some alternate explanations that are otherwise plausible.

In addition to these statistical analyses, we employ a systematic content analysis of online message boards and support groups for men who have lost their jobs or lost income relative to their spouses. These qualitative data are used to supplement the quantitative analyses, helping to shed light on the lived experience of the broad trends that we're examining.

Each chapter includes several sets of analyses, generally from multiple data sources. All the associated tables and figures have been compiled by the authors. The intent is to use multiple methods and multiple data sets to triangulate our findings. By testing our theoretical claims with a number of different operationalizations, data sets and techniques, we can make a much stronger case than we would otherwise be able to.

While the details of these analyses may be of interest to some readers, we know that not everyone wants to look through regression tables and diagnostics. Therefore, basic information about the data, techniques, and findings of each analysis is given in the main text, and the technical details appear in the Methodology Notes in the Appendix. Thus, the Methodology Notes contain all the information other researchers would need to replicate the analyses; the main text focuses on the story the data are telling.

THE STRUCTURE OF THIS BOOK

Our exploration of how men respond to gender threat comes in five analytical chapters, and a final chapter that sums up what we've found. Generally, the analytical chapters follow men into different areas of their lives, such as home and work, before broadening out into a study of larger political and social issues. We then use the results presented in these chapters to discuss how men's gender identities seem to be changing, and the conclusions we can draw across these areas.

In Chapter 2, "Mad Men at Work," we look at how men respond to gender threat in the workplace. We show that various measures of gender identity threat—like differences in gendered unemployment rates—serve as leading indicators of changes in reported sexual harassment and discrimination. However, these changes do not seem to lead to increases in other forms of harassment and discrimination. These findings add to our understanding of sexual harassment and discrimination, further demonstrating that they're not just about entrenched sexist attitudes, but are attempts by men to bolster their own threatened gender identities.

In Chapter 3, "Men and Politics," we explore the political effects of gender threat in men. Using a variety of techniques, including survey experiments and longitudinal data on political attitudes, we show that when men face gender identity threat, they tend to hold more conservative political views, and favor male candidates. This makes sense: as gendered political issues have become more prevalent in American society—and as more previously ungendered issues have become gendered—politics has become a potent way for men to express their gender identities in the face of threat. This chapter also reinforces the finding, which has been described for other behaviors as well, that men with different political and social views respond to gender role threat in very different ways. Thus, there are alternatives to hegemonic masculinity, and we find that men with liberal political views tend to become more liberal in response to gender threat.

Chapter 4, "Sexual Orientation and Gender Identity," takes this investigation further by examining how men view their gender identities, and how raising even the prospect of nonbinary gender and sexual identities can serve as a threat to those identities.

Chapter 5, "God, Guns, and Pornography," looks at other actions that men may take to bolster a threatened gender identity. In general, these are actions that can signal masculine identity to the individual, or to those close to him. Notably, some are also considered social issues of some concern. For instance, we find that men in US states with relatively high levels of ambient gender threat are more likely to consume certain types of pornographic materials, especially those seen as especially demeaning to women. Even though this is generally a private activity, it serves to symbolically reinforce male dominance for the individual consumer of the material. Similarly, we find that states with higher levels of gender role threat see related increases in firearms purchases, as measured through FBI background check data, and that the same states see subsequent increases in affiliation with conservative and traditional denominations.

In Chapter 6, "Alternate Masculinities," we bring together the evidence from the previous chapters to show that all the pressures discussed here push some men to embrace alternate masculinities, moving decidedly away from hegemonic masculinities. Some examples of these alternate attitudes and behaviors include increased time spent on childcare and cooking, more liberal political attitudes, and increased attendance at nonreligious social events. These alternate masculinities show the adaptability of men, and their ability to forego hegemonic masculinities in favor of new masculinities that are better suited for the current social and economic environment.

In the last chapter, "The Future of Men," we summarize our findings, discuss the policy implications and future directions for research that they suggest, and also apply our findings to groups that we haven't studied. The idea is to take this phenomenon of men trying to bolster a threatened gender identity and to examine it from all sides. Men's lives aren't constrained by the boundaries of academic departments, and so neither are our analyses. Too often, studies of gender have been conflated with studies of women, but as we hope to show, men are far stranger and far more interesting than they have been given credit for. Men's struggle with their gender identities isn't an issue just for themselves and their families but an ongoing activity that's shaping our political and social worlds.

CHAPTER 2

MAD MEN AT WORK

In 1997, the first year that the US Equal Employment Opportunity Commission (EEOC) released detailed data on formal complaints of sexual harassment in the workplace, it logged 16,000 such reports (monthly data for the smaller number of cases for which the race/ethnicity of the respondent is available are presented in Figure 2.1). (Data from earlier years are also available, but in highly aggregated form.) In 2017, the most recent year for which data are available, that figure had fallen to 9,600, a decline of more than 40 percent over 20 years. Such a drop seems like something worth celebrating; but to understand what's happening, it's necessary to understand why workplace sexual harassment is happening in the first place.

With the #MeToo movement, sexual harassment has once again come to be afforded attention in the news media. While harassment has been present in the political and social discourse at least since the Clarence Thomas confirmation hearings in the early 1990s, it has received much more attention since the 2016 presidential campaign and revelations about the behavior of a number of prominent men. For most Americans, though, harassment at their individual workplaces is of greater concern than the activities of celebrities, such as Harvey Weinstein and Louis C.K., and moguls, and not least, politicians. Men don't leave their gender identities behind when they come into work, and sexual harassment is one way in which some men demonstrate their masculinity. As such,

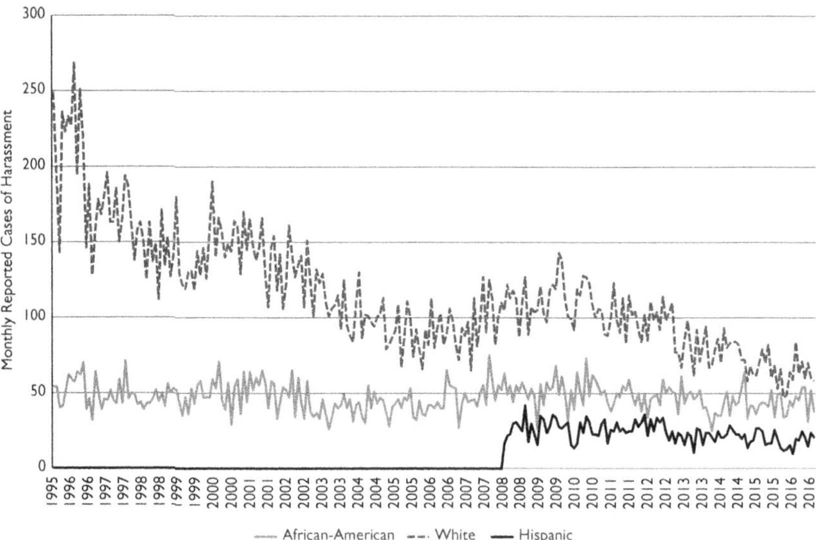

FIGURE 2.1: Women's Sexual Harassment Reports by Race or Ethnicity of Complainant: 1995–2016.
SOURCE: BuzzFeed data.

threats to their gender identities make men much more likely to engage in harassment; so as men perceive threat, harassment is likely to increase. One of the puzzles in the data then, is why harassment doesn't seem to have increased, even as men experience increasing levels of gender identity threat.

Today, nationally representative surveys find that about 25 percent of women report having experienced sexual harassment in the workplace, a figure that's broadly consistent across multiple studies (US Equal Employment Opportunity Commission). However, when women are asked about specific behaviors that constitute sexual harassment—such as sexual coercion or unwanted sexual attention—the reported rate of harassment increases to about 40 percent, likely because the women did not previously know which specific behaviors constitute impermissible harassment. Despite the ubiquity of sexual harassment in the workplace, McCann, Tomaskovic-Devey, and Badgett (2018) find that 99.8 percent of women who experience sexual harassment in the workplace never file formal charges. This may to some extent be due to fears of retaliation from employers (Stainback and Tomaskovic-Devey 2012; Berrey, Nelson, and Nielsen 2017).

The EEOC defines sexual harassment as unwelcome sexual advances, requests for sexual favors, and other verbal or physical harassment of a sexual nature. Harassment can also result from employers creating a hostile work environment by, for instance, making disparaging remarks about women in general. While the law does not prohibit jokes or teasing, these actions can constitute harassment if they continue or are so severe they constitute a hostile or offensive work environment (US Equal Employment Opportunity Commission 2018). Our use of the EEOC definition is not in any way intended to discount experiences of sexual harassment that do not meet it: as Schultz (2003) notes, sexual harassment is both a legal issue and a lived experience. However, owing to the nature of the data we are using, we rely on the legal definition. Note also that sexual harassment is legally and conceptually distinct from gender harassment, in which women are subjected to hostile behaviors at work that aren't tied to sexual interest, such as the use of gender-oriented slurs, which is also relatively common in the workplace (Cortina and Magley 2003).

What does sexual harassment actually look like in the workplace? We can see some vivid examples of it in Beth Quinn's study of "girl watching" at work (Quinn 2002). This study is particularly important because it looks at how masculinity shapes the performance of workplace sexual harassment. Looking at one Southern California electronics design and manufacturing company, Quinn focuses in on an activity that the workers call "girl watching": male employees gathering together to ogle female workers and discuss their bodies and how they're dressed. The male employees considered this to be harmless fun, and told Quinn that it has positive effects, increasing bonds between employees, and even functioning as a team-building exercise. Of course, female employees aren't included in the "harmless fun," as they might get offended or upset. Women are the central components of the activity, but it's based on the assumption that women are passive objects in the interaction. How they might feel about being ogled by their co-workers isn't part of the discussion.

Quinn finds that the men engaging in this activity don't see it as sexual harassment, but still worry about the consequences of being caught at it. These male workers have apparently had enough sexual harassment training to know that what they're doing is against the rules and to know there may be repercussions if they're caught, but they engage in the behavior anyway. These men are making what amounts to a private distinction between what they're doing, and real, or bad, sexual harassment. As far as they're concerned, no one is being hurt by their behavior unless the women find out about it—and if that were to happen, the real victims in their view would be the men themselves, who would be in trouble without considering themselves to have done anything to merit it.

Importantly, this girl watching doesn't seem to be about sexual interest: these men aren't generally trying to pursue sexual relationships with the women involved. Rather, the audience for their comments is the men they have gathered with. The public display of commenting on women's appearances serves to reinforce their own heterosexual masculine identities, and to demonstrate that masculinity to the men around them. In this way, the behavior of these men in the workplace is little different from the behavior of men who visit strip clubs (Erickson and Tewksbury 2010) or hit on women in bars (Grazian 2007). Gender, as Judith Butler (1988) has argued, is a performance: these men are performing masculinity to other men, showing the others not what the individual performers think is masculine behavior but what they think the other men will think is masculine behavior. At the same time, these men are demonstrating their masculinity to themselves, silencing any inner doubts about their masculine identities through the affirmation of other men.

The men in Beth Quinn's research saw girl watching as a harmless activity, yet this everyday activity they used for bonding and team- making resulted in harassment for women in the workplace. Many studies of sexual harassment point to male workers seeing sexual harassment as a problem of other workplaces and other workers, not themselves. Sexual harassment is so endemic, that like fish not seeing the water that they're swimming in, these men don't consider their own actions to be problematic, or see the ways in which masculinity displays might harm women in the workplace.

This sort of sexual harassment, in which masculinity displays are built into the structure of the workplace, is evident in the analyses Yasemin Besen and Michael Kimmel (2006) carried out in a study of depositions made by 110 Walmart employees, both former and current. These depositions were part of one of the biggest sex discrimination cases ever brought against a corporation. Even though the overall lawsuit proved unsuccessful, the sworn statements made by the plaintiffs show the impact of masculinity displays in the workplace, and how they actually play out. For instance, the plaintiffs reported that lunch meetings were held at strip clubs, or at restaurants like Hooters. Sites like these allow male workers to assert their masculinity and heterosexuality to other males in their workplace through a shared appreciation of scantily dressed (or undressed) women, but such displays almost necessarily leave out female co-workers. Like the women in Quinn's research, women who complained about these issues were seen as the problem, told that that they didn't have to go to the meetings if they didn't want to, and that they were causing problems for everyone by complaining about what the male workers saw as harmless bonding activities. Participation in these activities was seen as critical, though, for promotion and advancement opportunities, and staying away from them meant not only that women didn't get promotions but also that they often weren't even told about opportunities for them.

The harms to women from this masculinity-contest work culture were felt directly as well. Women who objected to this culture were accused of not being team players or of being prudes. The managers and supervisors argued that going to strip clubs was a team-building activity and that while participation was optional, women's refusal to be part of the team would be reflected in their evaluations. Yet having such team-building activities not only hurts women but also makes the assumption that all male employees enjoy strip clubs, or at least the opportunity to use strip clubs to assert their gender identities.

Such studies demonstrate the deep ties between sexual harassment in the workplace and men's struggles to reinforce their masculinity. Similarly, University of Toronto researcher Jennifer L. Berdahl (2007) shows how "uppity" women become the targets of sexual harassment. In three different studies, she finds that women who display traditionally masculine characteristics such as being dominant, independent, and assertive are more likely to be targets of sexual harassment in the workplace. Women workers who deviate from traditionally feminine roles and are seen as gender nonconformists are more likely to experience sexual harassment. If sexual harassment were about sexual interest, we might expect that women's displaying masculine-coded behaviors would lead to a lower incidence of sexual harassment. But workplace sexual harassment is about assertions of masculinity, and since assertive or dominant women may pose a threat to the masculinity of their male co-workers, their behavior is likely to trigger sexual harassment, as men seek to prove their gender identities to other men, and to themselves.

Nijole Benokraitis and Joe Feagin (1995) argue that this sort of discrimination against women through male and masculinity-oriented managerial cultures is especially difficult to root out, because it is invisible to the decision makers. Masculinity competitions and displays are so deeply entrenched, so integral to the culture of some workplaces, that even the women disadvantaged by them may not see the problem. We think of sexual harassment in the workplace mostly as individual actions carried out by bad actors, but it's more commonly the result of smaller acts informed by a larger workplace culture that privileges masculinity and masculinity displays. It's the culture of masculinity displays, of attempts by men to assert a masculine gender identity in the workplace, that leads to the more obvious forms of discrimination.

Unlike most of the previous research on sexual harassment in the workplace, our study takes a macro-level approach, looking at the large-scale trends in sexual harassment complaints, and how they're related to gender threat among men. If masculinity is an ongoing struggle and performance, and sexual harassment is often used by men to reinforce their gender identities, what happens when the economy changes, and men see their economic primacy threatened?

By examining the dynamics of workplace sexual harassment in the United States over the past 20 years, we can test findings about sexual harassment that have arisen from the existing micro-level research, and look for the effects of societal-level factors on reports of harassment. While sexual harassment is a societal issue, most of the research on it has looked at individual workplaces or small cohorts of victims: this work is valuable, but it's like carrying out case studies of a disease. Eventually, you have to move on to the epidemiology and study the population effects and the totality of the factors involved. Case studies reveal instances of how a disease spreads, and suggest what might combat it, but you need epidemiology to understand what drives it and what heals it. Workplace sexual harassment is a social phenomenon, and we need a societal-level view to really understand it.

The most compelling explanations of workplace sexual harassment come from the masculine overcompensation model (Willer et al. 2013), which posits that men react to potential loss of relative status by carrying out extreme forms of masculinity. For instance, Cassino (2018) finds that men who are merely told that women are increasingly likely to earn more money than their husbands (whether that is true in their case or not) became more likely to support Donald Trump in the 2016 US presidential race, and less likely to support Hillary Clinton. Similarly, men who lose income relative to their spouses adopt more conservative views on political and social issues like affirmative action and abortion, doubling down on conservative male dominance views in the face of a threat to their economic status (we present more data on this and related phenomena in Chapter 3). Such threats also lead men to overestimate their own height (Cheryan et al. 2015), hold negative attitudes about gay men with less masculine self-presentations (Glick et al. 2007), think about physical aggression (Vandello et al. 2008), put more effort into a handgrip strength test (Funk and Werhun 2011), become more supportive of war (Willer et al. 2013), spend less time on housework (Besen-Cassino and Cassino 2014), and make more muscular virtual avatars for themselves (Lee-Won, Tang, and Kibbe 2017).

This overcompensation behavior has been repeatedly linked directly with sexual harassment. Kevin Weaver and Theresa Vescio (2015) subjected participants to a gender knowledge test, and gave them feedback indicating that they were relatively masculine or feminine. Men who were given masculinity-threatening feedback became more likely to accept group-based inequality, and more likely to deny that other groups—gay men and women, in this study—were subjected to discrimination. Weaver and Vescio were able to show, through an experimental design, that when men's masculinity was under threat, men became more accepting of both social inequality and discrimination against disadvantaged women and gay men.

Anne Maass at the University of Padua (Italy) and her research team found that threats to men's dominance and gender identity led men to be more likely to sexually harass women (Maass et al. 2003). In this study, male students at the University of Padua were told they were participating in a study of visual memory and group dynamics, in which they would share images with other students and be asked to remember the images that had been shared. Each participant was seated at a computer terminal, in a small room with no other terminals or obvious observers, and told that he would be working with two other students, who were in different rooms. He was introduced to his two co-workers on the task through a chat function. All three of them were then asked to write a few sentences about themselves, what they were studying, and what they enjoyed doing in their free time. The first co-worker introduced himself as a male student, in fairly neutral terms. The second co-worker introduced herself either as having stereotypically feminine interests (wanting to be a schoolteacher and raise a family), or as being a feminist (studying economics, not worried about raising a family, and involved in the feminist movement). What the participant did not know was that the two coworkers weren't real and these responses were preprogrammed.

Then the task began. The participants were told to pick photographs from a wide variety of folders on their computer screens, labeled with themes (like "nature," "animals," "models," and "porno"), and then to pick which of the 110 images present they wanted to share with their co-workers. They were also told they would see the images shared by their co-workers, and that they would all be tested on their ability to remember these pictures. In the first rounds, both of the virtual participants shared fairly innocuous pictures, but matters soon turned. The male co-worker shared a hardcore pornographic image; these images had been selected by asking a different group of male university students to rate which images women would find offensive. This led the female co-worker to object, messaging the other two that the photo was disgusting, and asking them not to share such images. The male then messaged the actual participant, telling him that he should send pornographic images as well. Whatever the actual participant did, the male co-worker kept sending pornographic images, and the female co-worker stopped objecting.

After they had shared several rounds of pictures (and without any memory test), the real participants were told the true nature of the study, and sent home. Maass and her colleagues found that participants who had been paired with a co-worker they thought was a feminist sent more pornographic images than those who had been paired with a more stereotypically feminine co-worker. In this case, researchers were able to create a toxic environment of sexual harassment in the lab, and found that it was being driven entirely by men looking to assert themselves to another man in the face of a potentially "uppity" woman.

All of these results support our overarching theoretical argument about masculinity, and how men choose to go about reinforcing it. Sexual harassment is about men signaling their gender identity to themselves, and to other men. Some men might be generally more anxious about their gender identities, and more prone to needing these sorts of behaviors in order to assert their gender identity, while others may do so only under conditions of gender threat (and others, hopefully most, wouldn't do so at all). As we'll discuss more in later chapters, the exact way in which men express their gender identity varies widely by the environment they find themselves in, so it makes sense that men in environments where sexual harassment is more prevalent would be more likely to engage in it. Essentially, men are looking for socially acceptable ways to express their gender identity, and in some workplaces (like the one Maass and her colleagues simulated in their study), sexual harassment is perceived to be socially acceptable.

Many of the workplaces that breed sexual harassment seem to be pervaded by a toxic, gendered competition between men, what Berdahl and her colleagues have labeled a "masculinity contest culture" (Berdahl et al. 2018). In such workplace cultures, male employees frequently call into question the masculinity of other male employees, and challenge them to prove their gender identities. This sets up a pattern of escalating challenges between male employees, who are simultaneously questioning the masculinity of their peers, and seeking to outdo them in whatever way the others are proving their masculinity. Female employees are the most obvious victims of such environments, but male employees who don't engage in the contest culture are also likely to be marginalized at work, and may quit or lose their jobs.

So, in certain environments, men are likely to be more prone to sexually harass women, but we would expect this tendency to be exaggerated when men are facing higher levels of gender identity threat. These threats might take the form of workplace-specific threats, like increased status among women in the workplace (McLaughlin, Uggen, and Blackstone 2012; Chamberlain et al. 2008; Stainback, Ratliff, and Roscigno 2011), but they could also arise from societal changes, like economic threat. To the extent that sexual harassment functions as a gendered display of power and dominance, we would expect men to engage in more sexual harassment when they face economically threatening conditions.

While most threat may come at the personal level—earning less than a spouse, having a female manager—larger scale factors can also induce some degree of threat in male workers. Here, the unemployment rate seems a reasonable proxy for economic strain and threat. Past studies show a strong relationship between the perceived threat of unemployment and poorer psychological and physical health (Burgard, Brand, and House 2009; Burgard, Kalousova, and Seefeldt 2012; Benach et al. 2014), lower reported happiness (Di Tella, MacCulloch, and Oswald 2001), and increases in bullying and aggressive behavior in the workplace (Cortina and Magley 2009; Roscigno et al. 2009). Simply put, unemployment, or the threat of it, has been linked with stress and undesirable workplace behaviors, making it an indicator of strain and threat to economic status. As such, conditions of higher unemployment—experienced by workers as being threatened with personal job loss, knowing more individuals who have lost their jobs, or hearing about job losses through the media—are likely to lead to greater aggregate levels of economic threat. This connection between employment status and masculine identity has been made explicit in some recent research. Michniewicz, Vandello, and Bosson (2014) find that US men believe others will see them as "less of a man" if they lose their jobs, believe that the loss of gender status will be larger than US women believe it will be, and overestimate the extent to which others will perceive the loss of status. That is, even though not everyone perceives a strong link between men's gender identities and their employment status, these men do see a link, and thus, any threat of unemployment is a threat to their masculinity.

While all the existing data about gender threat are from individual-level studies, our data on threat are entirely on the macro-level, which may seem to be at a remove from the experiences of individuals. If we were trying to predict individual reports of sexual harassment, it would probably be inappropriate to make use of macro-level indicators, but our analyses look at the overall number of EEOC harassment reports in a given place, or time, or within a demographic group. While we cannot say that any macro-level indicator will induce a sense of threat in any individual, we can be confident that higher macro-levels of threat will lead to increases in the overall levels of threat experienced within a given population. This might not lead to one particular instance of reported sexual harassment, but may well lead to an overall greater prevalence of harassment behavior.

EEOC REPORTS OF SEXUAL HARASSMENT

To track reports of sexual harassment, we make use of three EEOC data sets: the first contains publicly released annual data reports, which include all types of harassment and discrimination and are broken down by the type of discrimination reported. The second contains state-based EEOC data, which display the national data broken down by the state (or territory, including Washington, DC) in which the reports were made (see also the analysis in Hersch 2018), and not including Fair Employment Practices Act reports, as these may include related but different information. All our state-based analyses use these data. The third data set contains the EEOC records on sexual harassment reports from October 1995 to August 2016, made available through a Freedom of Information Act (FOIA) request made by the news website BuzzFeed (yes, the one with all the quizzes). After BuzzFeed finished its initial reporting on this material, it made the data set available to other researchers, a boon given that these data are far more detailed than those found in the EEOC annual reports. The BuzzFeed data include the exact date of each filing, allowing us to analyze below the annual level provided in the public reports and to apply some individual characteristics of the women making the complaints (age, racial and ethnic background, and national origin) and of the company (number of employees and industry) where the harassment occurred. However, this granularity comes at a cost: rather than being broken down by state or territory, as in other EEOC reports, the data supply only national-level statistics, as individual cases might be identifiable in states with few reports. All told, nearly 160,000 cases of sexual harassment reported by women are included in the BuzzFeed data. (We excluded the relatively small number of cases—about 6 percent—reported by men.)

We aggregated each of these data sets into time series data. For the BuzzFeed data, we aggregated individual cases by the month of the report, as well as by the age of the complainant, her racial and ethnic background, and the size of her employer. For the EEOC data, we disaggregated the annual-level data by the state or territory in which the report took place. In both cases, the resulting variables consist of the number of harassment claims in a category (racial, ethnic group, or age category, or state, for instance) in a month (for the BuzzFeed FOIA data) or a year (for the EEOC data).

It's important to note that all these data sets on reported sexual harassment combine two theoretically separable constructs: actual sexual harassment in the workplace and reports of sexual harassment. It is entirely possible for the amount of reported harassment to change owing to a change in the likelihood of reporting rather than a change in the underlying rate of sexual harassment, and vice versa. We would argue not only that the number of reports of harassment is itself an important indicator, as it drives policy responses and official statistics, but also that there is little reason to believe women have become *less* likely to report sexual harassment over the last 20 years, indicating that observed declines in reported harassment are more likely due to changes in the underlying rates rather than changes in women's propensity to report harassment.

In addition, because we are looking at the dynamics—that is, the change—in sexual harassment complaints made to the EEOC, we do not need to assume that the EEOC is a perfect, or even an unbiased measure of workplace sexual harassment in the United States. Since we are looking at *changes* in the number of reported cases, all we need from the EEOC data sets is that they are consistent, and sufficiently large to allow for variance.

In this case, consistency means that the EEOC data are measuring the same thing over time. Ideally, it would mean there is some underlying stochastic process that results in some unknown (but very small) proportion of women who experience workplace harassment reporting it to the EEOC. So long as that proportion remains relatively stable, changes in the number of reports will reflect changes in the underlying number of workplace sexual harassment cases. The most likely threat to this consistency would be an increase in the likelihood that women would report harassment to the EEOC (as might result from the #MeToo movement, which took place after the data analyzed here were first reported). To the extent that we see an increase in the number of sexual harassment reports, it would be problematic, as the increase could be due to an increase in the underlying rate or an increased likelihood of reporting. However, because it seems that the likelihood of reporting has, if anything, increased over the years, to the extent that we observe a decrease in EEOC reports, it would mean the observed decrease is *understating* the actual decrease in the underlying harassment rate.

In addition, it is necessary that the EEOC sexual harassment numbers be large enough to allow for both positive and negative movement. If the reporting rate is so low that there are frequently zeroes in the data set, we would not be able to distinguish between stability in the underlying amount of sexual harassment and a decrease, as they would be observationally equivalent. However, given the number of reports made on an annual, and indeed monthly, basis, this is rarely an issue. Where it does occur, as in sexual harassment reports from US territories such as the Marshall Islands and Guam, where there are frequently zero reports in a month or a year, we excluded these data from our analyses.

We understand that this question of unobserved underlying rates of sexual harassment versus reporting rates is a major concern, and we have taken pains to establish, whenever possible, that we are looking at changes in the underlying rates, rather than in reporting. But given that we are observing, in general, decreases in reported rates of workplace sexual harassment, a change in reporting would call our findings into question only to the extent that women have become markedly *less* likely to report harassment over the past 20 years, something that has no basis in scholarly research on the subject.

Our analyses also require us to use an indicator of economic conditions. Scholars have used many indicators to measure economic conditions in the United States over time: the performance of the stock market, real wages, and inflation, for instance, but we focus on the unemployment rate. We selected this indicator because unemployment has the greatest direct effect on individual workers, and increases in unemployment rates are likely to cause the greatest threat to workers.

Finally, we should note again that all the analyses discussed here are based on data gathered prior to the start of the #MeToo movement in late 2017. It is entirely possible that #MeToo's encouragement of speaking out has led to an increase in women's making formal reports of sexual harassment, or even a wholesale shift in the dynamics of the reporting of sexual harassment; however, determining this will have to wait for a later analysis. The advent of #MeToo and the potential it has to shift the dynamics of reporting make the analyses we present here more urgent, as they will help to establish the baseline against which the effects of the #MeToo movement can be judged.

SEXUAL HARASSMENT AND UNEMPLOYMENT RATES

When we combine our data sets for unemployment rates and reports of sexual harassment made to the EEOC, we see a strong relationship between them. (For the full details of this and other analyses in this chapter, see the Methodology Notes.) Regardless of how we specify the economic threat—either as overall unemployment rates or as the change in unemployment rates—higher levels of unemployment correspond with more reports of sexual harassment from women. For instance, if the unemployment rate is at 9.1 percent in a month, rather than at its mean of 7.4 percent (one standard deviation above the mean), we would expect that reported sexual harassment would be about 5 percent higher in the following month. When the unemployment rate rises—regardless of where it was initially—we find that sexual harassment reports in the following month do increase significantly.

While it's always possible that some extraneous, uncontrolled, factor is confounding the relationship between the two variables, our use of lagged predictor variables does at least remove the possibility of reverse causation. We cannot mathematically exclude the possibility that something else is driving both numbers, but it would have to be some factor that drives unemployment now and sexual harassment later, which seems unlikely. In addition, we can be certain that we are not seeing reverse causation because this same lag ensures the Granger causality, establishing that, in the absence of a time machine, sexual harassment cannot be driving unemployment rates (even if, in many cases, women quit their jobs to avoid sexual harassment: see McLaughlin, Uggen, and Blackstone 2017).

Our statistical models allow us to reach two conclusions about the relationship between unemployment and reported sexual harassment. First, periods of higher unemployment correlate with periods of higher reports of sexual harassment to the EEOC. Second, increases in unemployment at time one correlate with increases in reported sexual harassment at time two. While these effects are not enormous, they explain much of the variance in the dependent variable, and are consistent with a world in which random factors are the main driver of month-to-month changes in reports of sexual harassment but factors like the stresses caused by increased economic strain play a role as well.

It might be argued that the unemployment rates are looking at overall economic strain, not just the strain experienced by men, and indeed, in later chapters, we'll look at alternate measures of strain that try to target men more closely. However, very narrow measures of unemployment are not appropriate for looking at workplace behaviors, because they're necessarily counting men who aren't in the workplace and, thus, can't harass anyone there. Moreover, while economic strain may well be experienced by both men and women, it's almost entirely men who are carrying out the harassment. Although sexual harassment claims are brought to the EEOC by men, most of their reported sexual and gender harassment comes from other men, especially when the complainant is gay (McGinley 2016; McDonald and Charlesworth 2016). While economic strain is certainly hitting everyone, it has not led to increased reports of women engaging in sexual harassment.

THE INTERSECTIONALITY OF WORKPLACE SEXUAL HARASSMENT

The decline in reports of workplace sexual harassment has not been evenly distributed across US women. While there has been a marked decline among white women, the number of reports of sexual harassment has stayed fairly constant among African-American women, even as the composition of the working population has shifted to become less white and older. While this difference is suggestive—perhaps men are choosing to harass women of color, rather than white women, because they feel they're more likely to get away with it—there are too many moving parts in the data for us to be sure. Still, it's important to acknowledge that sexual harassment impacts different groups of women in disparate ways.

While the effects of sexual harassment are well documented, research has started to emphasize an intersectional approach to the study of sexual harassment, highlighting differences in which workers are most likely to be harassed. Single women are more likely to experience sexual harassment as are highly educated women (De Coster, Estes, and Mueller 1999) and women in positions of power (McLaughlin, Uggen, and Blackstone 2012).

It seems reasonable in our current society to expect that women of color would experience greater levels of sexual harassment. As Linda Kalof and her team argue: "because sexual harassment is about power, we would expect less powerful people (e.g. women, minorities and younger individuals) to be particularly vulnerable to harassers" (Kalof et al. 2001). While McCann, Tomaskovic-Devey, and Badgett (2018) have found that women of color are less likely to be fired in retaliation for sexual harassment reports, feminist researchers more generally have called for an intersectional analysis of harassment. Many have argued that it is necessary to examine race, gender, class, and intersecting categories in order to understand oppression (Chafetz 1997; Collins 1990, 2000; McCall 2005; Buchanan and Ormerod 2002; Murrell 1996; Texeira 2002; Welsh et al. 2006). Still, scholars working in this area have based their findings almost entirely on micro-level analyses of the experiences of individual women, or women in individual workplace cultures, making clear the need for a macro-level analysis of the intersectionality of sexual harassment behaviors.

Research has shown that other demographic factors also play a role in understanding sexual harassment. Citizenship status (Hondagneu-Sotelo

1997; Arat-Koc 2001; Glenn 2000a; Welsh et al. 2006), ethnicity (Morris 1996; Berdahl and Moore 2006), and race (Mansfield et al. 1991; Yoder and Aniakuda 1996; Kalof et al. 2001; Welsh et al. 2006; Tester 2008) of women play a role. While earlier studies found no difference in the rates of sexual harassment of women of color (Gutek 1985), later studies have found evidence for differential rates of harassment (Welsh 1999; Williams, Giuffre, and Dellinger 2004) and have pointed to the complexity of intersectional systems of domination and of race, class, and gender (Collins 1990; Glenn 2000a; West and Fenstermaker 1995). In that vein, scholars have found that race and gender are intertwined in the harassment of women of color in the workplace and are not theoretically and methodologically separable, referring to "gendered racism" and "racialized sexual harassment" (Welsh et al. 2006; Banneriji 1995; Buchanan and Ormerod 2002; Texeira 2002).

CHANGES IN REPORTING, OR IN UNDERLYING RATES?

But are these reporting rates reflecting changes in actual rates of sexual harassment or in the likelihood of reporting? Again, we would argue that the amount of reported sexual harassment is also intrinsically important, but the data offer some clues. Looking at the ways in which reports of sexual harassment have changed can help to establish that changes seen over time are not so much changes in the likelihood that women will report sexual harassment as they are changes in actual harassment.

This distinction—between actual harassment and reports of harassment—is important not just for tracking increases and decreases but also and mainly because sexual harassment often has enormous consequences for the victims. Researchers have found that sexual harassment amounts to *systemic trauma* (Fitzgerald 2017) for women in the workplace, with consequences for victims that include depression (Friborg et al. 2017; Houle et al. 2011), burnout (Takeuchi et al. 2018), anxiety (Mushtaq, Sultana, and Imtiaz 2015), and even post-traumatic stress disorder (Avina and O'Donohue 2002; Sojo, Wood, and Genat 2015).

Some of the best work examining the impact of sexual harassment on its victims comes from Heather McLaughlin, Christopher Uggen, and Amy Blackstone (2017), who looked at a cohort of women in St. Paul, Minnesota. These women had been part of a longitudinal study that tracked them from high school through early adulthood, and McLaughlin and her colleagues were able to use the study's data to see how experiences of harassment affected and possibly derailed the personal and professional lives of the victims.

They found that experiencing sexual harassment is, among other things, a source of financial stress for women and interferes with their career goals. Harassment often leads women to quit their jobs in order to get away from a co-worker or a hostile environment. These work interruptions, in turn, leave women at an economic and professional disadvantage for years afterward, as they miss out on promotions, and when they do manage to find a new job have to start over at the new workplace. They also miss out on recommendations from supervisors or co-workers who may have been complicit or unsupportive, and experience a reduction in the professional networks available to them. Spelling these effects out in economic and professional terms may still underestimate the human cost of harassment. In their study, McLaughlin and her co-authors report talking to women who are desperate to get away from the harassment, even at devastating personal cost. One talks about how she doesn't care that she can't afford to quit, that she'll live without electricity if it means she doesn't have to go back to the workplace.

So the question of whether we're looking at changes in actual harassment or just in reports of harassment matters. But we necessarily don't have reports of unreported harassment, so we have to address the question indirectly, something that the BuzzFeed data set, which lets us look at differences in the number of reports by the size of the company, allows us to do.

Suppose that the reduced rates of workplace sexual harassment observed in the data are entirely due to a change in reporting. That is, the total amount of harassment is staying the same over time, and women are just becoming less likely to report the harassment. Of course, this interpretation ignores all the research that seems to show the opposite, that women have become more likely to recognize and report harassment over time, but what would the patterns in the data look like if this interpretation were true? We would expect to see the biggest decrease among women working in companies where it is easiest to report harassment: that is, in the largest companies. In smaller companies, women may have no alternative to working under a particular manager or with a particular set of co-workers, and perhaps no human resource department to deal with harassment issues and ensure legal protections for victims. We would thus expect women in these smaller companies to be less likely to file a complaint. In larger companies, though, women should be more willing to file a complaint, given at least the possibility of being shielded from retaliation (even if that possibility isn't always realized). So, if women who were choosing to report harassment in the 1990s are simply choosing not to today, we would see the biggest shift in the workplaces where they were most likely to file in the first place: in the biggest employers.

Breaking down the reports over time by the size of the employer (using the BuzzFeed data set), we find that reports of harassment at the largest companies (those with 500 or more employees) have remained fairly stable over time, with the mean number of reports per month dropping by only about 12 percent between 1996 and 2016 (see Figure 2.2). The bigger drop comes in companies with between 15 and 100 employees, where harassment reports from women dropped by about two-thirds over the same period.

Reports of harassment at companies with less than 500 employees dropped at about the same rate as at the largest employers. This is not what we would expect from a drop in the likelihood of reporting: if that were the case, we would see the biggest drops at companies with the most employees, where the barriers to reporting are lower. If anything, it likely became easier to report harassment at smaller companies over the period

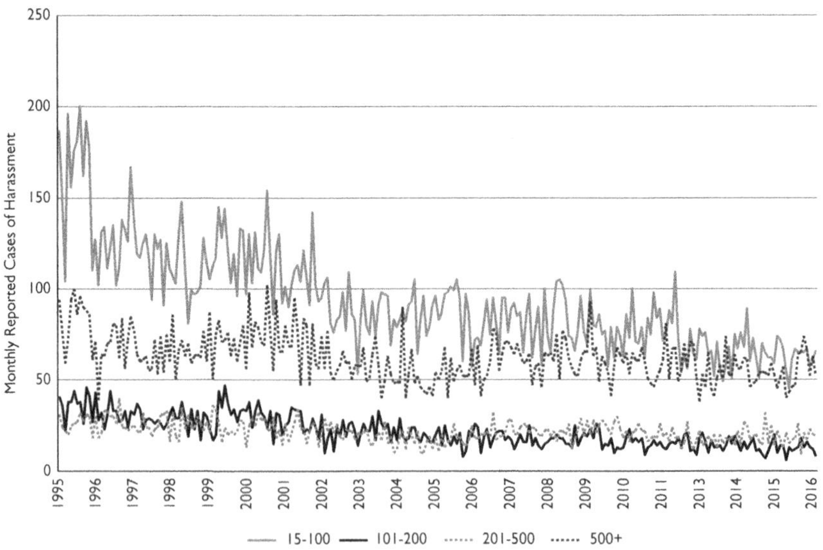

FIGURE 2.2: Reports of Harassment by Size of Employer: 1995–2016.
SOURCE: BuzzFeed data.

covered in the data, and this likelihood supports the notion that we're observing a drop in actual harassment behaviors, rather than simply a drop in reporting.

All of these figures are complicated, of course, by changes in the composition and nature of workplaces and employees. Employees have generally gotten both older and less white over the period covered by the EEOC data, and they have acquired increased information and access to human resource departments, and these developments have likely made women more likely overall to report harassment than they were in the past (even if that gain is from a very low baseline). If we had observed an increase in harassment reports over time, it could have been argued that that increase reflected a change in the likelihood of reporting, rather than a change in the underlying rate of the behaviors. However, it would be hard to sustain such an argument in the face of the declines in reports shown in the data.

There's also a strong theoretical reason to expect that broad-based economic threat would result in increased rates of harassment. The anxiety produced by economic threat, in the form of high unemployment rates, leads men to look for ways assert their masculine gender identities. Sexual harassment is one way in which they can do so, and so harassment increases along with economic uncertainty. The exact degree of that increase is hard to pin down, owing to the low reporting rate: all we can be sure of is that the increase in actual harassment is orders of magnitude larger than the increase in formal reports of harassment.

It also seems likely that the decrease in sexual harassment seen over time in the data is of a larger magnitude than is evident from the measurements. Because of increased information among women as to what constitutes actionable harassment, and the increased availability of resources, it seems likely that women have become *more* likely to report harassment over the past 20 years. This means that the decreased number of reports likely reflects the reporting of an increased percentage of harassment; the fact that the number of reports is falling means that the reduction in incidents of harassment is outpacing the increase in reporting. The numbers tell a story of substantial reductions in workplace harassment of women over time, but the situation is likely even better than that.

Of course, this evident progress raises another question. It's not as though men have experienced less gender identity anxiety in the years since 1996, and as we'll see, many of the behaviors that men use to compensate for threat have become more common over the years. So why has the level of workplace sexual harassment fallen?

The key to this likely has to do with the flexibility of responses to gender identity threat among men. Masculinity is a malleable concept. Even faced with similar types of threat, men have many ways of asserting their masculinity in response. The same factors lead some men to embrace certain religious practices, some to use certain types of pornography, and likely, some to do both. So, while the dynamic of a threat to masculinity leading to a response is stable, the form of the response is shaped by all sorts of factors, including the perceived acceptability of the response in the man's immediate social environment. As evidenced by the "girl watching" study and others, workplace sexual harassment by men is enabled by the behavior of other men in the workplace, and what's perceived to be acceptable. Just as women in the United States have become more cognizant of what constitutes sexual harassment over the past 20 years, so too have men. There are likely many workplaces where some forms of sexual harassment that had no repercussions 20 years ago are no longer considered acceptable. The men in those workplaces have a choice: they can continue to engage in what's now an unacceptable behavior—and many of them are—or they can find some other way to assert their masculinity. These alternative responses aren't necessarily going to be any more socially desirable, but the reduction in workplace sexual harassment certainly is.

These analyses make use of previously under-utilized macro-level data to test the expectations of previous, micro-level studies of sexual harassment in the United States. The major limitation of such an approach is that it relies on complaints made to the EEOC, so the figures may change as a result of either a change in the underlying rate of sexual harassment or in women's propensity to report sexual harassment. It is our stance that the reported rates are, themselves, worthy of inquiry, as they form the basis for official statistics and the information given to lawmakers looking to address the issue. However, as we have discussed, our analyses of differential rates based on race, age, and employer size strongly suggest that the movement in the number of reports of sexual harassment is due to changes in underlying rates, rather than changes in reporting propensities. While the likelihood of reporting sexual harassment over time has likely changed, there is no reason to expect, nor have any scholars in our reading of the literature proposed, that women have become *less* likely to report sexual harassment over the last 20 years.

Also, we would expect that women with relatively more power in society would be the most likely to see an increase in the likelihood of reporting sexual harassment, but it is white women who have seen the biggest decline in reported sexual harassment. Similarly, if changes in the propensity to report are driving changes in EEOC findings, we would expect the biggest declines to occur in large employers, where women are more likely to have access to official channels for their complaints, but the decline in reports is largest among medium-sized and small employers. None of this is to say that the propensity to report has not changed over time, but rather that any such changes run counter to the observed macro-level trends, implying that our results are likely *underestimating* the actual effects.

It might also be the case that women are more willing to report sexual harassment when the unemployment rate is relatively high, as reporting may look easier than finding another job. However, we expect that any such effect would be swamped by the number of women who would choose not to report harassment for fear of losing their job in a difficult labor market.

Our analyses also make the case that sexual harassment is an increasingly racialized phenomenon. Even accounting for demographic changes in the composition of the female workforce in the United States, African-American women have become increasingly more likely than white women to report sexual harassment. The analyses that look at changes in the number of complaints by state, size of employer, and age also help to build the case that this difference is in underlying rates of sexual harassment, rather than in differential likelihoods of reporting.

Our analyses also show how national economic factors, like the unemployment rate, can impact the rate of sexual harassment of women in American workplaces. About one-third of the change in workplace sexual harassment reported to the EEOC can be attributed to changes in the national unemployment rate in the previous month. When the unemployment rate goes up, producing greater societal strain and a need to assert dominance, reported sexual harassment goes up as well. When conditions for workers are better, and the unemployment rate falls, so too do reports of sexual harassment. These results, too, strongly suggest that changes in the numbers EEOC reports are driven by the actual incidence of sexual harassment, rather than changes in the propensity to report. Given that women (reasonably) report fear of retaliation for reports of sexual harassment in the workplace, if we were seeing a measure of the propensity to report harassment, we would expect that figure to *decline* when the unemployment rate rises, rather than increase.

From a theoretical perspective, these findings help to establish that gender threat can lead men to look for compensatory behaviors in the wider world, outside the relatively intimate spaces of the household. If men were acting to express their gender identities only in the home, and largely to their families, it might well be seen as a matter of less importance for society. People work out all sorts of anxieties and stresses at home, and while these behaviors are often socially undesirable, they are also private. But here, we've seen that men are bolstering their gender identities through behaviors in the workplace as well, in ways that negatively impact people outside their families, and in ways that often have victims.

Our analyses have shown that increased levels of economic stress lead to increased levels of sexual harassment. Even though we're relying on reports of sexual harassment—and we know that the overwhelming majority of sexual harassment incidents don't lead to complaints—we can use what we do know to strongly suggest that we're looking at real changes in harassment, rather than changes in reporting habits.

Research that has looked at individual workplaces and also work that has simulated work environments to try to uncover the causes of sexual harassment, like the previously described study carried out by Maass and her colleagues, also point to the importance of workplace culture. As we've already seen, and will show again and again, men have access to a myriad of behaviors for reinforcing their masculinity in the face of threats. They can deal with gender threat through politics, through religion, at the gym: so why do it in the workplace, where they may well face consequences for their behavior? In part, this choice may arise from the expectations and behaviors of other men. Think of the rather typical example of girl watching presented by Quinn. If one man in the workplace started ogling female co-workers, and commenting on their appearances, he would likely be in trouble. But if he's among a group of men who are doing the same, and who have been doing it without consequences for some time, failure to join in could itself become a source of gender identity threat. Would the participants in Maass' study have sent pornographic images to a woman, over her objections, had they not been egged on by another man? Perhaps, but certainly not nearly as frequently. This implies that threat is a necessary, but not sufficient, condition for harassment, and more work needs to done to identify why harassment flourishes in some workplaces but not in others.

Our results support the notion that sexual harassment in the workplace is about men establishing power and dominance over women, and establishing their gender identities to themselves and to other men. When men feel threatened—in the case of our examples, by economic factors out of their own control—they become more likely to engage in workplace sexual harassment. In this, the causes of sexual harassment that have been identified in the micro-level literature seem well supported in the macro-level data.

This is not to say that threatened men are indiscriminate in their sexual harassment behavior. Men may be carrying out harassment in order to ameliorate threatened gender identities, but they're doing so when and where such harassment is a culturally accepted way of achieving this relief, something we'll see with other masculinity-boosting behaviors in later chapters. As it has become less acceptable to sexually harass women in the workplace, men seem to have shifted to other behaviors that are acceptable, or are at least less likely to get them into trouble.

This finding also answers one of the puzzles arising from our argument about the sources of harassment. If sexual harassment in the workplace is about asserting masculinity in the face of external threats to men's gender identities, and if men are more threatened now than in the past, why hasn't sexual harassment *increased*, rather than decreased? We would argue that the increased likelihood of consequences for harassment and the decreased acceptability of harassment in workplace cultures have led men to find other ways to work out their gender identity anxieties. In the past, sexual harassment may have been a relatively costless way for men to demonstrate masculinity to themselves and other men around them, and men took advantage of it. But as the costs and acceptability of harassment changed, men have adapted, shifting to other behaviors that are as costless now as harassment was in the past.

We also haven't addressed the #MeToo movement, mostly because sufficient data were unavailable. But we think that #MeToo has to be thought of as being separate in important ways from the data we're drawing on.

Because nothing like the #MeToo movement happened during the decades that produced the data we're looking at, we can make a plausible case that changes in reported harassment during that time are representing changes in actual harassment. But #MeToo, if it means anything, means that many women who otherwise would not have reported harassment have now chosen to do so. As such, the case that reporting rates have stayed approximately stable falls apart, and the change in the number of reports—and there was a significant, through uneven increase—would then be about reporting and not about underlying rates of harassment. An increase in reporting is certainly a good thing, as it's likely to lead men to be less likely to engage in workplace sexual harassment, but it presents a challenge for the data analysis.

While our data have allowed us to uncover a lot about why sexual harassment in the workplace happens, and how it's changed over time, the most important conclusion we can offer is that there are ways to deal with the issues we've identified. Harassment is not a problem of just a few bad apples or something that happens in one industry, in one workplace, or with one culture. It is a societal issue, and approaches to studying it should be as wide as the problem itself is.

CHAPTER 3

MEN AND POLITICS

Given that the 2016 US presidential election was decided by the vagaries of the Electoral College and small shifts in votes in a few states, it can be difficult to draw conclusions about American society from the outcome. However, we can learn a lot from what happened during the campaign, and what it revealed about the relationship between gender roles and US politics. Simply put, the possibility of a female president, and of Hillary Clinton in particular, represented a grave threat to the gender identity of many men, a threat that Donald Trump was able to capitalize on. However, gender threat didn't suddenly appear in US politics in 2016; it has had an impact on the political views held by men for many years. What's different about the 2016 US presidential election—and the political environment that followed it—is that gender has now become a more important part of the discourse, which has led to a greater role for gender identities in political attitudes and behaviors.

Men might have chosen not to vote for Hillary Clinton for many reasons: she had a political record going back decades in which people found issues they could use to justify opposition to her, and media coverage of alleged improprieties certainly didn't help. So how can we be sure that opposition to her was based on gender threat and not some other factor? This is where experiments are especially valuable: if individuals are randomly assigned to two groups, and there are no differences in how the groups are treated except for an experimental treatment, and the two groups are different at the end, the difference must almost certainly be the result of the experimental treatment.

We'll make use of a number of survey experiments and other studies to show the impact of gender identity threat on men's political stances, but the most direct evidence comes from an experiment embedded in an otherwise standard telephone survey of voters in New Jersey, a state that leans strongly Democratic, and in which Clinton was expected to have an advantage because of the proximity to her New York City home and her previous role as one of New York's US Senators. (See the Methodology Notes for this chapter for the full details of all the research described here.) At the time of the survey, in the spring of 2016, the Democratic primary was still being contested by Vermont Senator Bernie Sanders, and even though it seemed very unlikely that he could win the nomination, his presence in the race allowed us to include a series of questions asking about match-ups between Clinton and Trump and between Sanders and Trump.

But before respondents were asked about the match-ups, half of them were made to think about gender role threat. Respondents who were married, or living in marriage-like relationships (a civil union, or a long-term partnership without marriage, for instance) were asked this question: "There are an increasing number of American households in which women earn more money than their husbands. How about your household? Would you say that your spouse earns more than you, less than you, about the same, or is your spouse unemployed?"

Of course, we don't expect people to answer this question honestly. We know, from government earnings data, that about one-third of men in the United States earn less money than their wives, but in past surveys, only about 15 percent of men say that their wives earn more (women seem to be a lot more open to saying that they earn less than their spouses). It's possible that the respondents don't know their exact relative incomes, or that they have a very broad view of "about the same," or that they're simply lying, but the answers and the reasons for them really don't matter. The goal of the question is to create some degree of gender identity threat in the male respondents, to raise the fact that many men in the United States are earning less than their wives, and thus raise the prospect that they, too, might earn less.

The men in the survey who didn't get the threat-inducing question favored Hillary Clinton in a match-up against Donald Trump by a 16-point margin: a big gap, but not too surprising in a strongly Democratic state. But the men in the threat condition favored Donald Trump in the same match-up by an 8-point margin, an overall shift of 24 percentage points, and random assignment means there's no explanation for the difference other than exposure to the threat condition (see Figure 3.1).

Of course, if that were the only result, it would be possible that the threat was simply leading respondents to prefer Republican presidential candidates—but remember, the respondents were also asked about a potential match-up between Trump and Sanders. In that match-up, the priming (raising the specter of men earning less than their wives) had no significant effect. The threat induction led male respondents to be more likely to support Trump, and less likely to support Clinton, but not less likely to support a male Democratic candidate who was seen as even more liberal than Clinton (see Figure 3.2).

The gender threat prime also served to reduce support for Trump among women, across both conditions, perhaps because it made them more likely to consider his views on issues important to many women.

In Chapters 1 and 2, we've shown that gender threat leads men to embrace compensatory attitudes and behaviors to reinforce their masculinity to themselves and others. In this chapter, we look at how voting and political attitudes can serve this role. Even a threat as nebulous as the

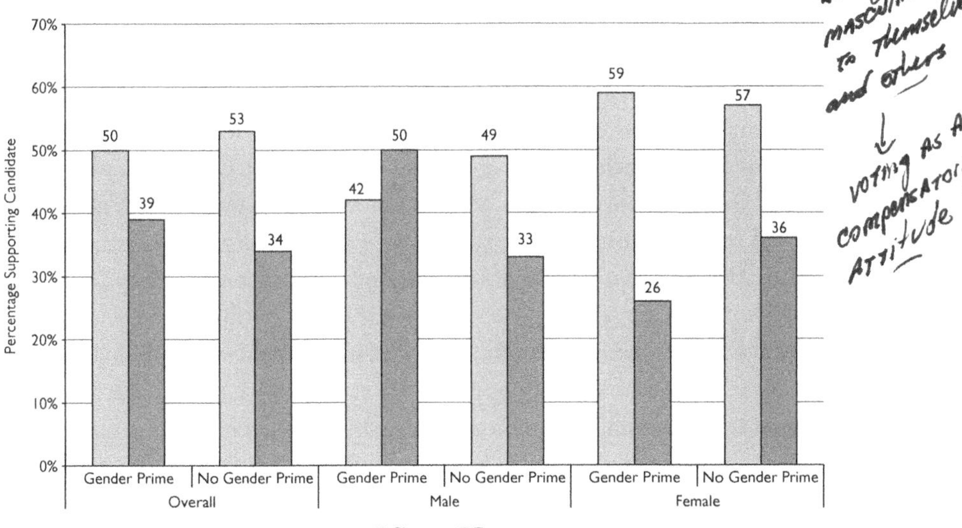

FIGURE 3.1: Effect of Gender Priming on Clinton-Trump Match-Up.

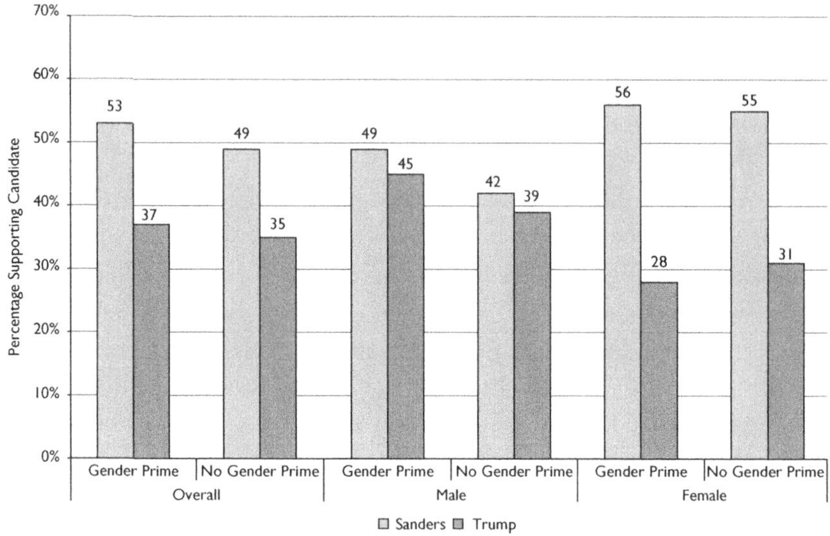

FIGURE 3.2 Effect of Gender Priming on Sanders-Trump Match-Up.

fact that a lot of women earn more than their husbands causes enough threat to make men more likely to express support for Trump in a match-up with Hillary Clinton. If that's the case, what other political attitudes might be pushed around by the perception of a threat to men's gender identities? How much of US politics is being driven by men seeking to assert their masculinity by holding certain views?

We're far from the first researchers to show a strong link between US electoral politics and male gender roles, though much of the past work has centered on the effects of stereotypes about men and masculinity. For instance, Meredith Conroy, a political scientist at California State University, San Bernardino, has written extensively about ways in which political media emphasize the importance of masculine traits in elections, while treating feminine traits as flaws or weaknesses (Conroy 2015). For instance, being aggressive—a stereotypically masculine trait—is seen as a strength on the campaign trail, and even in governance, while a stereotypically feminine trait like cooperation is seen as a weakness. Such gendering of traits becomes even more of a problem when narratives about elections highlight dichotomies, a tendency often leading to an election being framed as a fight between desirable masculine traits and undesirable feminine ones. Conroy's example is the 2004 Democratic presidential nominee John Kerry, who was framed as being feminine, despite his military service. After 2016, it became clear that this use of stereotypes would only be exacerbated in an electoral race between a man and a woman. However, while a discussion of the gendering of traits and candidates in the media is important to an understanding of US elections, the key insight for our purposes is the idea that a candidate's sex is secondary in importance to a candidate's gender. That is, male candidates aren't necessarily seen as masculine, nor female candidates as feminine, even though that's probably the default. Men subjected to a gender role threat didn't become more likely to support Trump because he was a man but rather because he was seen as a particular type of man, and by announcing their support of him, threatened men could assert their own masculinity. The same effect likely would not have occurred had Clinton been in a match-up with a male candidate perceived as having feminine qualities, like Kerry.

Work by Emily Carian and Tagart Sobotka of Stanford University seems to confirm this. In an experiment they carried out, men subjected to a hypothetical threat to their employment didn't become more likely to say they would support a male candidate for president, but *did* become more likely to say that they would support a masculine candidate (Carian and Sobotka 2018). Similarly, Monika McDermott, in her book on gender identity in American political behavior, shows the extent to which gender dominates the way Americans perceive the political parties, with more masculine traits—among both men and women—corresponding to greater support for the Republican Party (McDermott 2016).

This view of a source of support for Trump builds a compelling narrative. American men, owing to shifts in the economy or the perceived erosion of male privilege, experienced gender threat. This, in turn, led them to prefer a more masculine candidate, or at least to reject a female one.

The idea of masculine gender identity being threatened by a direct economic threat—especially for men earning less than their wives—runs throughout this book, but there simply aren't enough men suffering direct economic threat to account for the sorts of shift we saw in our original survey experiment. That experiment was designed to make men think about that sort of threat, but we then made use of a follow-up study, this time with questions included on a national survey, to see if less direct, more ambient threats had similar effects. In this second survey—carried out the month after our initial study—respondents were asked a series of questions about women's roles in society. These questions were designed not only to measure men's attitudes but also prime them to think about the loss of dominance among men generally, rather than any threat specific to themselves. Half of the respondents were given these questions before answering presidential match-up questions, and half afterward. The results were similar to the previous results, but showed signs of conditionality not present in the initial study. Among men perceiving that society is biased against men—the 22 percent of respondents who said that the media treat women *less* harshly than men—the prime reduced support for Clinton by 6 points in a match-up with Trump, while having no significant effect on support for Sanders.

While the results of the two studies are generally the same, it seems that priming men to think about the increasing status of women in society generally didn't lead all men to prefer a male candidate to Clinton in the general election. Rather, the prime seemed to be activating negative views of women among men who already saw some degree of gendered status threat. (See Figures 3.3 and 3.4.)

This makes sense: priming changes responses by making certain factors more or less relevant to the evaluation currently being made. If someone cares a great deal about abortion rights, and a survey asks a question about abortion right before asking about a match-up between candidates, abortion should weigh more heavily in the respondent's decision about

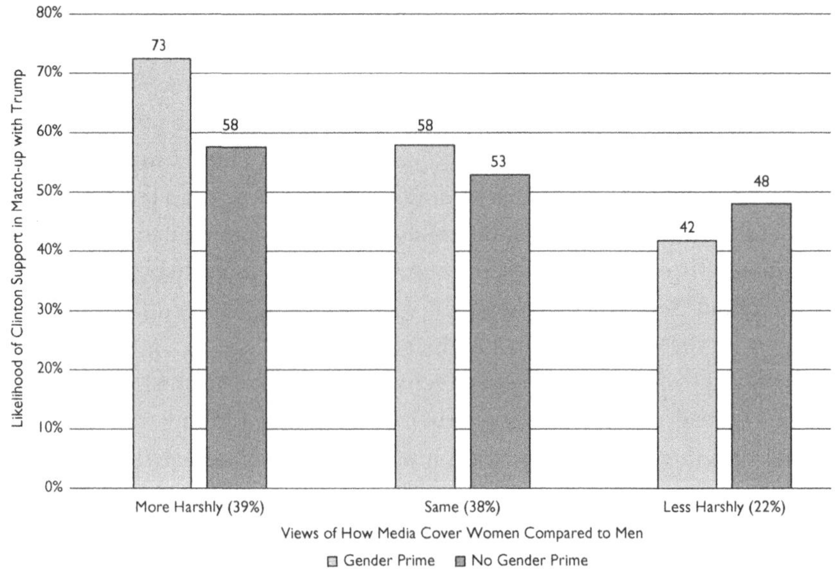

FIGURE 3.3: Effect of Ambient Threat Priming on Clinton-Trump Match-Up.

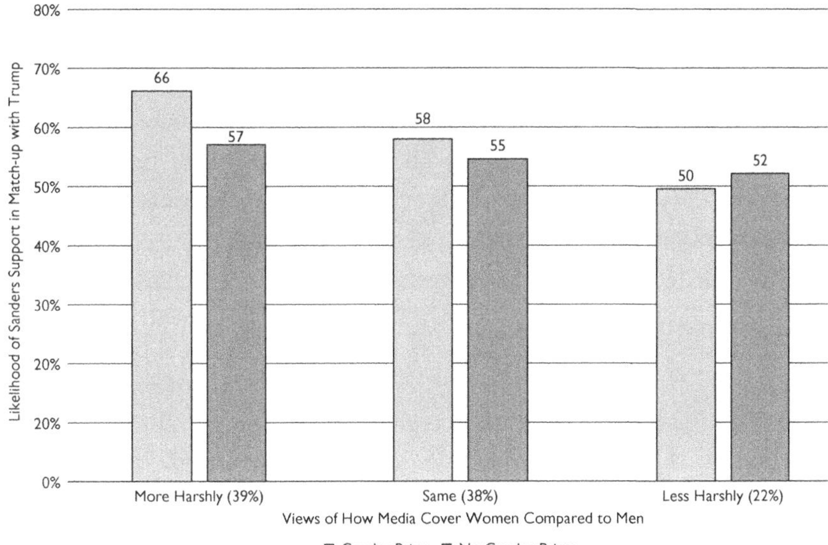

FIGURE 3.4: Effect of Ambient Threat Priming on Sanders-Trump Match-Up.

whom to support. However, if the respondent doesn't have strong views about abortion to start with, priming them to think about it probably isn't going to do very much. Similarly, having men think about threats to their gender identity, or threats to men's status generally, should affect preferences only among men who feel strongly about those threats to begin with.

Several open questions arise from these two studies. For one, why does it look as though the threat is impacting men, generally, in the first and not in the second experiment? That seems to be simply because the first study didn't directly gauge men's views of ambient threat. Since a plurality of men feel that men's roles in society are at least a little threatened, any analysis that lumps in all men together is going to find that this sort of priming has an effect across that group. Put another way, if the priming has a large effect on one group and no impact on others, in the aggregate it will look as though there's a small effect throughout all the groups; it's not until we divide the groups up that the actual impact is visible.

When we use indirect measures—in this case, the self-described political ideology of the respondent, expressed in the broad categories of liberal, moderate, and conservative—we see evidence of the same polarization in the first study as well. While priming men to think about gender identity threat leads them to become less likely to support a female candidate—or at least, Hillary Clinton in particular—it increases that likelihood among more liberal men. The movement against Clinton seems to have arisen entirely from the effects of the priming among conservative and moderate men, who swamped the liberals with their larger numbers.

While the data may seem to be saying that gender identity threat leads to men becoming more conservative, it's more accurate to say that gender identity threat leads to polarization among men, with conservative men becoming more conservative, and liberal men becoming more liberal. It's only because there are more conservative than liberal men that, on average, the effect tends toward the conservative side. This polarization effect shows up in several of our other analyses as well, and is one of the signs that men may be redefining their masculinity in new ways.

Other researchers have had similar findings about the role of threat and sexism in both driving and undermining support for Clinton in 2016. In their analysis of the 2016 US presidential election, Erin Cassese, a political psychologist at the University of Delaware, and Mirya Holman, a political scientist at Tulane University, differentiate between two kinds of sexism (Cassese and Holman 2019). Benevolent sexism holds that woman should be revered by men, but are too fragile to survive without men's protection. Differences between men and women are thought to be innate: women are simply better at some tasks (like housework and raising children) than men are, and should be encouraged to pursue such tasks, in what's sometimes called a separate spheres ideology. Benevolent sexists are likely to believe that they aren't sexist at all, as they don't dislike women—they're trying to help and protect them—they just think women should stay in the roles they're naturally best at. We measure benevolent sexism by asking respondents if, for instance, women should be cherished and protected by men. Hostile sexism, in contrast, holds that men and women are fighting for societal dominance, and any gain in women's rights necessarily comes at the expense of men's privilege. Hostile sexists are likely to engage in overt discrimination against women, and condone violence against them. In surveys, we measure hostile sexism by asking respondents, for instance, if women use men to try to gain power. In other analyses, we use a hostile sexism scale to measure sensitivity to gender role–based threat (see the Methodology Notes for Chapter 3 for this scale).

Cassese and Holman find that women in the United States display lower levels of benevolent sexism than men. While Democrats display somewhat lower levels of benevolent sexism than Republicans, the link of hostile sexism to political party is even stronger, so that Democrats are much lower than Republicans on hostile sexism. In the face of Trump's claim that Clinton was playing "the woman card," and relying on appeals to her sex, respondents who were high in hostile sexism became more motivated to vote against her, and those who were low in hostile sexism were effectively demobilized, becoming less interested in voting at all. Benevolent sexism had much weaker effects, with Trump's comments apparently causing anxiety among respondents high in benevolent sexism, as they might well oppose a female president—women should stay in their rightful places—but didn't like to see women attacked.

So, while sexism generally may be fairly widespread, the particular flavor the sexism takes matters a great deal. It is hostile sexism, more than its paternalistic cousin, that turned voters against Clinton, perhaps because hostile sexism sees powerful women as a problem for men. But while all these studies come to similar conclusions about how sexism worked against a female candidate in 2016, they all have one big confound: Hillary Clinton herself. With only one woman in the race, it's impossible to know if the effects seen were due to a female candidate, or due to that female candidate in particular. To see if threat has the same effects on support for other female candidates, we need to look at an election in which multiple women are running: for this we have the 2020 Democratic presidential primary election.

In examining this primary election, we draw on an online survey sponsored by Data for Progress (DFP), and carried out by a well-regarded, online survey house, YouGov. The survey was taken in the immediate aftermath of the first set of Democratic debates in the summer of 2019. To find out what characteristics voters valued, independently of the candidates, DFP used a series of randomly generated head-to-head match-ups between hypothetical primary election candidates. A set of traits, which carried no title but that included demographic characteristics and policy positions, accompanied each candidate. After reviewing each randomly generated match-up, respondents were asked which of the two randomly generated candidates they would prefer, which of the candidates could beat Trump in a general election race, and how motivated they would be to vote for each of the two candidates. The survey included five of these head-to-head match-ups between Democratic candidates, and the random assignment meant that some respondents saw a match-up between two female candidates.

The idea here was to use the match-ups between two women as a threat condition. When the choice was between two women—and the question was which the respondent preferred—none of the above wasn't really an answer. This meant that respondents who otherwise might never select a female candidate were being forced to do so. While subtle, this should be enough to present a degree of threat—in this case, a loss of male social dominance—that should lead to differences in later responses. Of course, in many cases, the respondent's next choice was between two male candidates, but we looked at those individuals who had to choose between two female candidates and were then asked to choose between a male candidate and a female candidate. If the threat really is an issue, men forced to pick a female candidate in one match-up should be more likely to pick a male candidate over a female one in the subsequent match-up.

But there's also a twist: respondents were also randomly assigned to a particular order of the demographic items, so some saw the race of each candidate first, some saw the sex of the candidate first, and so on. This means that the sex of the candidate was being downplayed—put at the end of the list of demographic traits—for some respondents, and relatively stressed for others.

When the sex of the candidate is stressed, men are 7 points less likely to pick the female candidate immediately after a choice between two female candidates (moving from 55 percent to 48 percent). Among women, there's no significant difference: when sex is stressed, women pick a woman in the subsequent match-up 52.6 percent of the time; when it isn't stressed, the figure is 53.5 percent. (See Figure 3.5.)

The fact that we see a significant change among men, but no change among female respondents, tells us that this isn't about the quality of the candidates, or any other gender-neutral explanation. But for confirmation, we can split the data up differently. For instance, we can look at the difference between liberal and moderate men (remember, this is a Democratic primary poll—there aren't a lot of conservatives in there). Among self-identified liberal men, stressing the sex of the candidate reduced support for female candidates after a two-female match-up by 5 points, from 57 percent to 52 percent. But among self-identified moderates, stressing the candidate's sex reduced support by nearly 11 points, from 51 percent to 40 percent. So, the threat seems to operate on both groups, but influences liberal men much less than it does more conservative men.

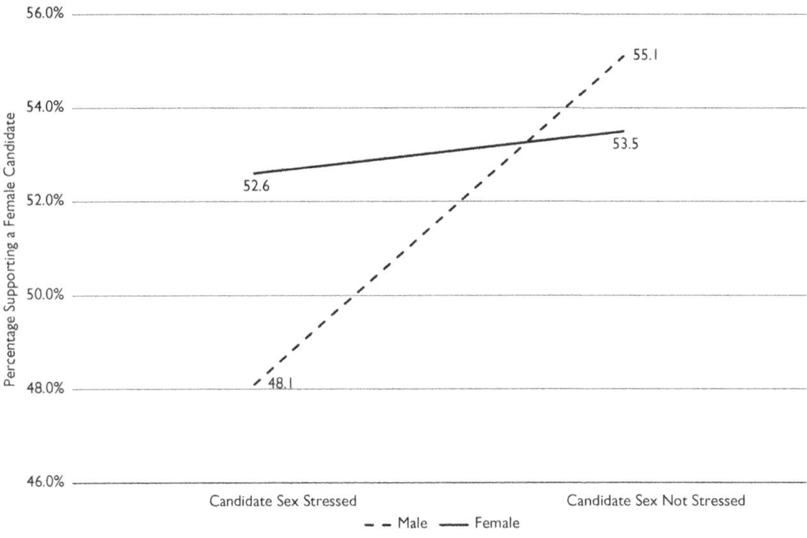

FIGURE 3.5: Support for Female Candidates, by Sex and Condition.

We can get at the issue even more directly by making use of a sexism scale embedded in the survey, which can be used to measure the extent to which men see threat to male dominance in society. Among men with low scores on the sexism scale (which asked about things like women using men to get ahead, and women being oversensitive to sexist comments), stressing the sex of the candidates reduced support for female candidates in the wake of all-female match-ups by about 5 points, from 60 percent to 55 percent. But among men with moderate or high scores on the sexism scale, stressing the sex of the candidates reduced support from 55 percent to 46 percent, a difference of 9 points.

So, the manipulation—randomly forcing respondents to choose a female candidate—reduced support for female candidates among all the groups that we would expect to be sensitive to gender role threat: men generally, non-liberal men, and men with moderate and high scores on a sexism scale. At the same time, it has small or no effects among groups that we wouldn't expect to be sensitive, like women, liberal men, and those with low scores on the sexism scale. In addition, the effect is larger among these groups than among men generally, supporting the idea that gender identity threat is hitting some groups harder than others.

The same experimental manipulation also reduced men's desire to vote for a female candidate. After asking which of the candidates in the match-up the respondent preferred, the survey asked how motivated the respondent would be to vote for each of the candidates in the match-up in a general election race against Trump. As you might expect, Democratic primary voters were, on the whole, pretty jazzed to vote for anyone who was running against Trump: on average, they gave the candidates a 7.1 on a 0- to 10-point scale. The sex of the respondent didn't change this overall figure much: men gave the male candidates a 6.96, and female candidates a 6.99. Women gave the male candidates a 7.03, and the female candidates a 7.13 (the higher mean scores for female candidates are likely driven by the higher quality of the average female candidate).

But when male respondents are asked to choose between two female candidates, their motivation to support female candidates in the subsequent match-up suffers. While men overall give themselves 6.99 points out of 10 on their motivation to vote for female candidates, after a match-up between two women, that motivation falls to 6.62. It also falls among female respondents—from 7.13 to 7.02—but that difference isn't significant.

This effect is magnified when we break out respondents by their sexism scores. Among men with a low sexism score, motivation to vote for a female candidate isn't impacted by having to choose between two female candidates: in fact, motivation even climbs, if insignificantly, afterward. But among men with moderate or high sexism scores, choosing between two female candidates dramatically reduces motivation to vote for a female candidate in a subsequent match-up: from an already low 6.85 to 6.40 points on the 10-point scale. Women with moderate and high sexism scores have lower motivation to vote for female candidates overall than less sexist women, but choosing between two female candidates does nothing to reduce that motivation further. (See Figure 3.6.)

This is exactly what we would expect from a threat manipulation: men who are already sensitive to gender role threat—as evidenced by their scores on the sexism scale—respond negatively toward female candidates in the face of that threat. Not only are they more likely to support a male candidate in the subsequent match-up, they're also less motivated to support a female candidate, even in a match-up with a president from the opposite party who's among the most unpopular major party candidates in history.

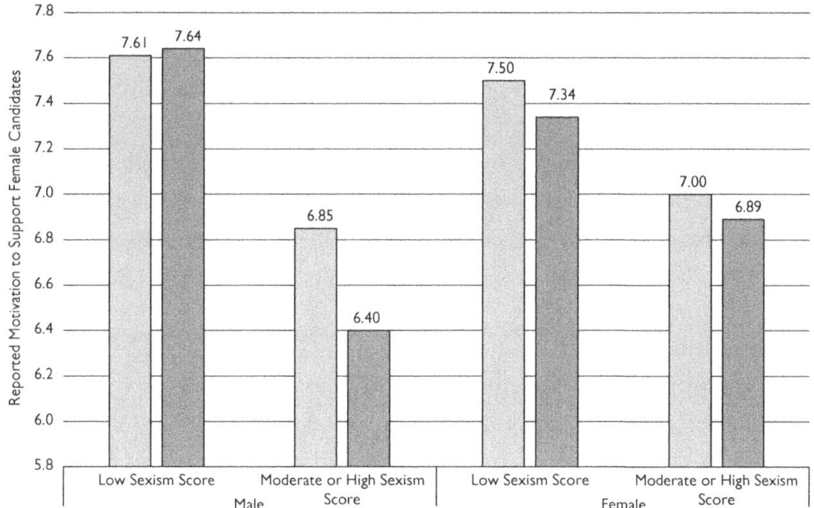

FIGURE 3.6: Effect of Two-Female Candidate Match-Ups on Motivation, by Sex and Sexism.

The Democratic primary electorate, like any other group of people in the United States, contains men who are sensitive to gender identity threat, and when that threat arises, they adjust their attitudes, to the detriment of female candidates. But these results also indicate that bias against female candidates—at least within the Democratic primary electorate—can be mitigated. When the list of a candidate's attributes stresses the sex of the candidate, men who have moderate or high scores on the sexism scale are 10 points less likely to vote for them. But those same respondents are only 5 points less likely to vote for the same female candidates when the sex of the candidate isn't stressed. Simply put, sexism drives responses more when the sex of the candidate is presented as being important. When other attributes, like race, ethnicity, or age are presented as being more important, voters don't think about the sex of the candidate as much, and are thus less likely to be driven by gender-based concerns.

One difference between these findings and those of the previous experiments is the lack of an opposing response among liberals. In other experiments, we found that priming with the gender role threat leads liberal men to be at least marginally more accepting of a female candidate, and in this experiment, there's no evidence of that. While less sexist and liberal men's likelihood of supporting a female candidate subsequent to choosing a candidate in a two-female match-up goes down less than that of moderate candidates, it still goes down, not up. One reason might be the difference between benevolent and hostile sexism. While hostile sexism has the strongest effects in driving down support for female candidates in the face of threat, benevolent sexism has been shown to have similar effects, with a smaller magnitude. Because the items used to measure sexism in this survey are all hostile sexism items, our group of "low sexism" men may well include some proportion of benevolent sexists, who are driving these results.

Most importantly, though, these results help us answer the question of whether gender identity threat turns some male voters against Hillary Clinton in particular or against female candidates more generally. In addition to being the first female major party nominee for president, Clinton has a long history of being attacked for comments that were perceived as overly ambitious for a woman. After all, one of her first forays into public awareness was the controversy over a comment she made in 1992, about whether a professional woman was suited to being first lady: "I suppose I could have stayed home and baked cookies and had teas, but what I decided to do was to fulfill my profession, which I entered before my husband was in public life." Her ambition, her role in the powerful, normally male position of Secretary of State, her feminism: all these traits could be reasons why Clinton would be a uniquely threatening candidate for men concerned about threats to their gender identity. After all, other female candidates, like the 2008 Republican vice-presidential nominee Sarah Palin, didn't inspire the same sort of sexist rhetoric that Clinton faced, like the 2016 campaign T-shirts reading "Trump that Bitch," or roadside signs warning against her "vagenda of manocide."

While Palin might serve as evidence that not all female candidates spur the same level of gender role–based threat in men, our analysis indicates that it does go beyond Clinton. While it doesn't differentiate between female candidates that might be considered more (Senator Elizabeth Warren) or less (lifestyle guru and officiant at Elizabeth Taylor's last wedding Marianne Williamson) threatening, the fact that our results apparently apply to a broad range of female candidates is itself telling. It seems that Democratic female candidates for president, at least, are punished by men looking to bolster a threatened gender identity, at least by those men most sensitive to that threat. Palin may well be the exception because of her explicit framing of herself as someone who was not a threat to male social dominance, in her repeated self-description as a "hockey mom," or her opposition to reproductive rights, or her assertions that her husband was dominant in their relationship. Even then, Palin (alongside Clinton) faced plenty of sexist backlash in the form of sexist memes and pornographic images and movies edited, or cast with lookalikes, to feature her. In the absence of more prominent female Republican candidates to compare her with, it's impossible to be sure.

While the framing of Clinton as some kind of radical feminist and threat to American manhood certainly drove some of the backlash, it's entirely possible that any female candidate who presents as being outside the norms of traditional femininity would face the same backlash. It's female candidates generally, rather than Clinton in particular, who present an opportunity for some male voters to assert their gender identities. As noted before, it seems that it's gender, more than sex, driving these attitudes.

Still, all of these studies—and much of the past work in this area—rely on experiments, in which researchers artificially induce gender identity threat in men. Researchers generally see experiments as the best way to establish cause and effect in scientific studies, but experiments leave open the question of whether their results hold up in the real world.

To dig into this, we made use of a panel study embedded in the General Social Survey (GSS), one of the largest high-quality surveys carried out in the United States. Most surveys are cross-sectional, meaning that they take a random sample of a population at one point in time, and compare the results from that sample with a different sample of the same population carried out at a different time. A panel study, in contrast, asks questions of the same people repeatedly, allowing researchers to see how individuals change their views over time. This makes it much easier to isolate causation: we can see what changes in people's lives tend to correlate with changes in their attitudes, in a way that's impossible in cross-sectional studies.

We were lucky that the timing of the panel study—running from 2006 to 2010—coincided with the Great Recession. This meant people had changes in their financial situations, leading many men to experience more economic threat than they would have in another period. The first wave of the survey took place in 2006, squarely before the Great Recession; the second wave during the initial period of the recession, in 2008, which disproportionately impacted men. During that second period, the male unemployment rate rose to more than 2 points above the women's unemployment rate for more than a year. That 2 percent difference represents millions of households in which men lost their jobs, while the women did not. Indeed, more than half of the men in the panel reported having a lower income, relative to their wives, more than in the first wave of the panel. Twenty percent of the men lost more than 25 percent of the relative income in the household, dropping, for instance, from contributing 60 percent of the total household income to 35 percent. About 8 percent of the men in the sample became unemployed between panel interviews, compared to about 6 percent of the women. By the third wave of the study (in 2010), this difference between men's and women's unemployment had largely receded, partially because of improving conditions for men, and partially because austerity measures in public sector jobs disproportionately hurt women.

In the study, respondents were contacted up to three times, at two-year intervals, and asked about their finances as well as about their social and political views: all told, 1,712 men, 742 of whom were married, gave responses in at least two of the waves. The fact that the same individuals were asked for information at multiple points in time means that we can track how changes in household relative income from one point in time to another point two years later correspond with changes in political views over the same time. This eliminates selection bias, a major problem in most studies looking at relative income. It's entirely possible that men who choose to marry women who make more money than they do, or who have the capacity to do so, are different from men who choose to marry women who don't make more money than they do. Indeed, at least one large-scale analysis has found that loss of relative income matters only to men who earned more money than their wives at the start of the relationship. Therefore, any analysis that looks at differences between the men who make more and the men who make less than their wives might be driven simply by preexisting differences between these two groups. By looking at the same men at different points in time, we can be more certain that the differences are driven by changes in the individual, rather than reflecting the difference between people who opt in to different types of relationships. While this wasn't a natural experiment—we have no reason to believe that losing income during the recession was randomly distributed across men—a strong relationship between losses of relative income and attitude shifts would be good evidence for a causal relationship.

Using this study, we looked at changes in attitudes on three political issues: government aid to African-Americans, access to abortion, and support for marriage equality. We selected these three issues because past studies had argued for links between them and men's gender roles. Government aid to African-Americans draws on issues of self-reliance, as well as social dominance, a trait that's been strongly linked to masculinity (especially among white men in the United States) in the past. Abortion views draw both on religious views as well as views about the role of women in society, and questions about marriage equality give male respondents an opportunity to express their views of gay men, and differentiate themselves from them.

In these analyses, we control for factors like changes in employment, marital status, and church attendance, as well as the age, race, and other demographic characteristics of the individual. Controlling for these factors means that we can be confident that any change in attitudes is due to change in relative income, and not due to other changes that might have gone along with it. For instance, losing income might make men go to church more often, and that might make men more likely to oppose abortion rights. Controlling for church attendance means that we can rule this out as an explanation for the observed change. Divorce, as it turns out, is the most important control: in addition to its effects on income, it has enormous impacts on social and political attitudes.

On two out of the three political issues, loss of relative income was associated with more conservative views among Republican men. For instance, Republican men who were at the 10th percentile of change in relative income (meaning a drop of 39 points in the percentage of income earned by them), were, on average, 0.25 points less supportive of abortion rights on an 8-point abortion scale at the end of the wave than at the beginning. Republican men whose income remained stable were only about 0.17 points lower, and those who gained income relative to their spouses were only 0.10 points lower, on average (see Figure 3.7, which breaks these findings down further by level of household income: low, moderate, or high). The pattern here is of men becoming more anti-abortion over time—owing either to aging or to changes in politics over the period studied—but loss of relative income accelerates this change. Importantly, these men came to hold stronger anti-abortion views even when their

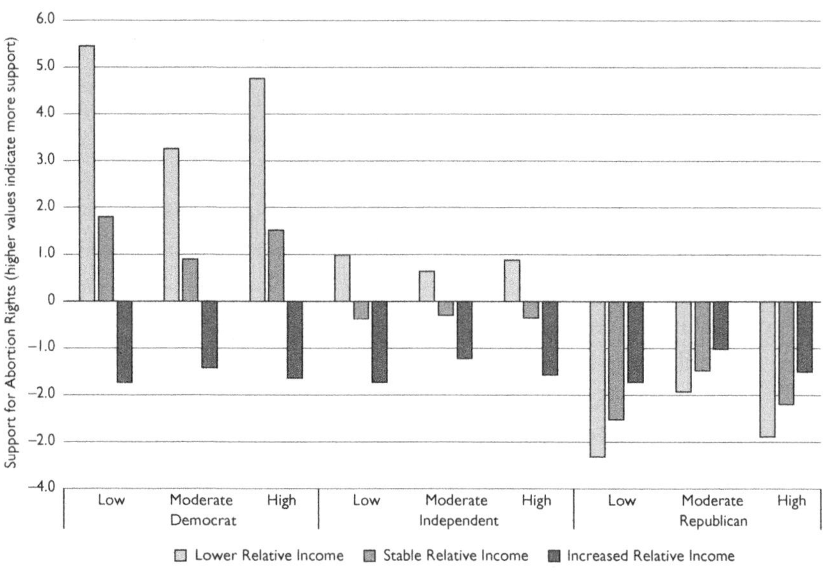

FIGURE 3.7: Effect of Income Threat on Men's Abortion Views, by Household Income and Party ID.

own income didn't drop: it was enough that their spouse earned more, decreasing their share of household income.

The results for support for government aid to African-Americans were even more striking. Republican men who lost income relative to their spouses were less supportive of the aid, with their scores dropping by about 0.10 points, while those whose income remained stable saw their support shift marginally in the opposite direction. Republican men who gained income relative to their wives actually became more supportive of government aid to African-Americans, by about 0.20 points. (See Figure 3.8.)

The findings aren't all so clear-cut. While loss of relative income has a significant impact on men's attitudes toward marriage equality, that shift was counteracted by other variables in the model, perhaps indicating that the effect of relative income loss was swamped by the enormous overall shifts in attitudes toward marriage equality that occurred over the course of the panel study.

Issues that aren't tied to dominance—like environmental policy—show no significant change tied to income loss once we control for change in overall political affiliation: however, becoming a Democrat or a Republican does shift these views. This implies that we're not seeing a general shift in political views but rather men changing their views on specific political issues in order to assert their masculinity in the political realm.

In addition, the absolute income of a household—how much money is coming into the household overall—doesn't seem to have a consistent effect, even though it might be thought that men in lower income households might face more threat from the loss of relative income. Despite this, though, the findings are consistent with the previous studies. Men who feel that their gender identity has been threatened, by specific threats like loss of relative income, or by more diffuse threats like a society they perceive to be biased toward favoring women, are changing their political views in response.

We shouldn't overlook the role of political independents in all of this. For the most part, Americans who claim to be independent actually feel affiliated with one party or the other, but have decided that declaring themselves a partisan is socially undesirable. So, while there are plenty of independents in the US electorate, most of them, when pushed, admit that they lean toward one party or the other, and most surveys treat these "leaners" as partisans (on many measures, they're stronger partisans than individuals who "weakly" associate with a party). However, in

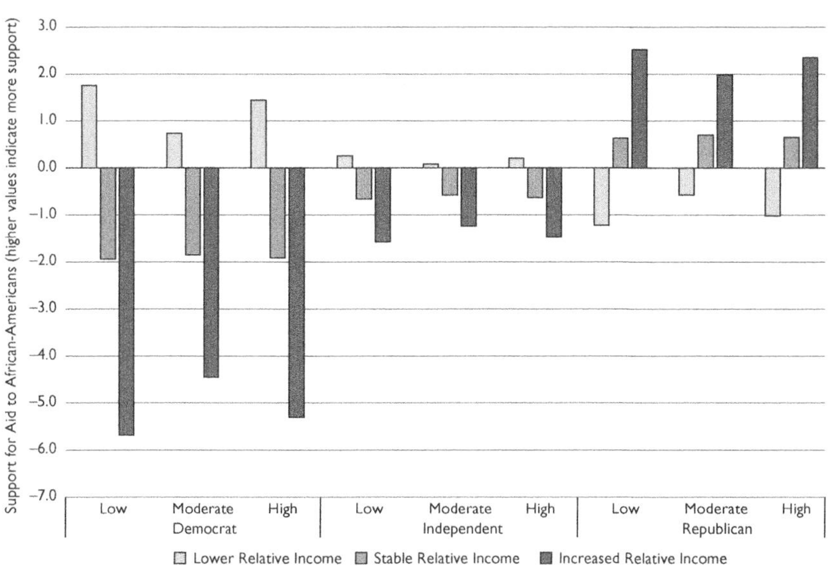

FIGURE 3.8: Effect of Income Threat on Men's Support for Aid to African-Americans, by Household Income and Party ID.

none of our issue questions do we see significant movement, one way or the other, among political independents: so what's going on? The most likely explanation is that while political independents are doubling down on *something* in response to gender identity threat, they're doing it in some nonpolitical area. After all, if they really are independent, they are, by definition, not tied into a particular set of political beliefs, so politics may just not be relevant enough to their gender identity to be a worthwhile expression of gender.

Also striking in these results is the extent to which liberal men show countervailing effects. Controlling for other factors, Democratic men who experience income loss relative to their spouses come to hold more liberal views on the issues we looked at, just as Democratic men in the survey experiments became rather more likely to vote for a female candidate when their gender identity was threatened. To make sense of this, it helps to remember that while there may be a hegemonic masculinity, a set of behaviors and attitudes that form the dominant societal idea of masculine gender identity, the gender identity of any particular man is likely to be much more nuanced. When their gender identity is threatened in some way, men respond by doubling down on an aspect of their masculine identity that they can fulfill, but which aspect they choose to double down on is determined by their own unique gender identity and the context in which they find themselves. So, while the dominant masculine gender identity in the United States might hold that dominance over women, racial minorities, or other groups is a masculine trait, individual men might associate being an ally to such groups with their own masculinity. As with conservative men, threats to masculinity are likely to make such liberal men double down on some aspect of their gender identity, but these threats may well serve to make them more liberal, rather than more conservative. On average, gender threat may be making men more conservative, but only because there are more conservative than liberal men to start with in the United States.

Of course, this is not an unalloyed positive, even for those who might favor liberal policy outcomes. Research on these latter sorts of masculinities has found that they're most likely to be held by members of privileged groups, like young heterosexual white men. These attitudes and behaviors can serve as an expression of identity for white heterosexual men whose identity is seen as the societal default, or as a way for men to distance themselves from what they recognize to be male privilege.

However, some, like Michael Messner (1993) or Tristan Bridges and C. J. Pascoe (2018), have argued that such liberal masculinity expressions have a dark side, as they tend to stigmatize the masculinities displayed by less privileged groups and to obscure continuing inequities. Messner, in particular, writes about meetings in the 1990s in which men were invited to share their feelings and vulnerabilities with each other in a supportive setting, to talk about the ways in which they felt that they weren't living up to the ideals of hegemonic masculinities. This all sounds good, but, as Messner points out, they may be rejecting the parts of masculinity that are bad for them personally, but they're certainly not rejecting male political and social dominance. Indeed, one of the selling points of these meetings was that being in touch with your feelings and connecting with other men would make you *more* successful in business, in society, and in your relationships. In essence, these men are trying to mitigate the costs of being on top in society, so that they can be happier—without having to actually move toward societal equality.

Politics, like sexual harassment, is a powerful way for men to symbolically express their gender identity. Not only do female candidates present a threat to men's social and political dominance, which may trigger gender identity threat in some men, but expressing opposition to female candidates seems to be a way for some men to assert their gender identities.

As we've shown here, while relative economic loss may be one of the most potent threats men face, it is far from the only threat that leads men to feel the need to assert their gender identity. Elections where choices are limited to two women are enough to trigger gender role threat, and some men, it seems, perceive a degree of gender identity threat ambient in society, a trait that we've measured with hostile sexism scales. Men who are high in hostile sexism—who see relations between men and women as a zero-sum game that inevitably has winners and losers—perceive a greater degree of threat than other men, and see it in situations that others may see as anodyne. Because of the different techniques we've used to suss out gender threat and responses to it in political situations, we've been able to see this conditionality in a way that isn't possible in some other analyses. It seems likely that the same sort of conditionality holds in other areas, as well, with some men becoming more supportive of female co-workers in the face of threat, for instance, even though we can't isolate such effects in the data. Such findings help us to build up the theoretical backdrop for all of our analyses: yes, men respond to gender threat by doubling down on aspects of their gender identity that they can fulfill, but some men are more sensitive to gender threat than others, and different men are likely to double down on different aspects of masculinity. In some cases, this may lead them to attitudes or behaviors that go in entirely the opposite direction of the modal response. Importantly, this is not random variation, where gender threat leads to one effect or an opposite effect for no apparent reason. Rather, we can measure the degree to which men perceive threat, and we can assess their likely response to it, by looking at predispositions like political views. More conservative men tend to respond in one way, whereas more liberal men are likely to respond in another way. Exactly how men make these attitudes fit into their idea of masculinity is a topic we deal with through qualitative analyses in a later chapter.

Our findings also help to identify the far-reaching political effects of the Great Recession on some men's political and social behaviors. Blaming the bad behavior of some men on "economic anxiety" has become a punch line in online discussions in recent years. In the wake of a resurgence of white nationalism, the idea that overt racism or sexism can be explained by a loss of income, or even just a loss of relative economic status, seems laughable. It isn't economic anxiety or fears of loss of relative status that lead men to become racist or sexist; it's that loss of relative economic status cuts to the core of these men's gender identities. When they believe they're losing status in society relative to others, they are, in their own eyes, less masculine, and as other research has shown, they overestimate the extent to which others feel the same way (Michniewicz, Vandello, and Bosson 2014). They wind up casting about for another way to assert their gender identities, and overt sexism or racism may seem like a reasonable way to go about doing that.

Of course, this argument isn't meant to absolve anyone for their bad behavior: there are many, many, ways to be a man, and some men have chosen to pursue some ways that may harm others or society. And we aren't discussing competing explanations of whether racism or sexism or economic threat is the major factor in certain behaviors: in many ways, all these motivations come down to the same thing.

CHAPTER 4

SEXUAL ORIENTATION AND GENDER IDENTITY

In the last chapter, we showed how threat to men's gender identities can lead them to adopt compensatory political attitudes and behaviors, using votes and statements of opinion to assert their masculinity. But in recent years, shifts in US politics have shown that, for many men, sexual orientation and gender identity (SOGI) have become intrinsically linked with political identity. This has become most obvious in the political conflict over allowing transgender individuals access to bathrooms that match their gender. This debate has seemed to embody the worst of American politics: with one side arguing that society should respect the preferred gender identity of transgender individuals, and treat, for instance, transgender men the same way as any other men, and the other side arguing that sexual identity is immutable, and that pretending otherwise puts vulnerable groups in harm's way, as sexual predators would exploit the rules to assault women and children in women's bathrooms. As happens so often in American politics, the two sides have been talking entirely past each other: proponents see the arguments about safety as utterly facetious, bad-faith efforts to deny rights to transgender individuals, while opponents don't see transgender people as being a group that deserves any regard under the law.

What's striking about this debate is the seeming mismatch between the ferocity with which it has been fought and the consequences of it for most people. Transgender individuals, by and large, already use the bathroom corresponding to the sex they present as, so non-transgender men have likely used a bathroom alongside a transgender man, and women have likely used a bathroom next to a transgender woman. There's no one checking birth certificates at bathroom doors, so except in narrow cases, like high schools, rules allowing transgender individuals to use the bathroom that they prefer wouldn't be likely to change anyone's behavior or experience of using a public bathroom. So, why the vitriol? As we'll show, merely mentioning nonbinary conceptions of sex or gender presents a threat to the gender identity of US men. Some men in the United States see recognition of transgender individuals, or of any nonbinary conception of sex or gender, as a threat to their gender identities, requiring the sort of over-the-top response that we've seen in other areas. Moreover, for men who assert strongly masculine gender identities, gender identity is tightly linked with political identity: among men, traditional conceptions of masculinity and Republicanism are so tightly linked as to be inseparable.

It may sound trite to say that "not all men" engage in the sorts of behaviors we've been talking about, but there is variation among men in both their gender identities and the importance of those gender identities to their overall conception of themselves. Social science researchers don't seriously think that differences in attitudes and responses are driven by sex. Instead, as Monica Schneider and Angela Bos (2019) put it: "Sex differences . . . require gendered explanations." In other words, an observed difference between men and women is likely a difference between masculine and feminine identities that isn't being measured. Some men pursue a completely masculine gender identity, while others are open to admitting that they have feminine traits as well. When it comes to political views, men who have a completely masculine gender identity are very different from men whose gender identities are more complex. It wouldn't be much of a stretch to say that the real gender gap in US politics is between men who hold a strongly masculine gender identity and everyone else: men who hold any other sort of gender identity generally have attitudes more similar to those of women than they do to the attitudes of these men.

Assertions of a completely masculine gender identity are closely linked with political attitudes on a variety of measures, a relationship that becomes clear when we take the opportunity to actually measure gender identity. Social science researchers have long understood that gender and sex are distinct constructs, but measurement, until very recently, hadn't caught up with this understanding. Gender is understood to be a multidimensional construction, with most people having a combination of masculine and feminine traits. However, in telephone surveys, the indicator called "gender" is often just an interviewer's best guess as to the sex of the person the interviewer is talking to, based on the voice. Non-binary response options—like menus on websites that allow respondents to choose from more than two sex categories—are an improvement over past techniques, but they still don't do a good job of measuring variation in sex and gender, which can be fluid and complex and doesn't fit into a pat category for many people.

The gold standard technique for measuring gender identity is the Bem Sex Role Inventory (BSRI; Bem 1981), in which respondents are asked to rate themselves (using a 7-point scale running from "Never or almost never true" to "Always or almost always true") on a variety of traits, such as "sympathetic," "forceful," and "aggressive," that are perceived as being relatively masculine or feminine. Respondents who say that they "always" display the feminine traits get a high score in femininity, but could also get a high score in masculinity if they also choose masculine traits as their traits. The BSRI is well-validated, and Fordham University's Monika McDermott (2016) has used it to analyze the link between gender and political attitudes in recent years, but it's too long to be included on surveys that aren't dedicated to it. To try to find a more efficient way to ask about gender identity, Canadian researchers Amanda Bittner of Memorial University in Newfoundland and Elizabeth Goodyear-Grant of Queen's College in Ontario have made use of a self-placement scale that asks respondents to position themselves on a 101-point scale ranging between total masculinity and total femininity (Bittner and Goodyear-Grant 2017a, 2017b).

Others, like sociologists Devon Magliozzi, Aliya Saperstein, and Laurel Westbrook (2016), make use of scales that, like the one we used, ask participants how they see their own gender identity, but supplement those scales with separate scales asking participants how *others* view their gender identity (what Magliozzi and her colleagues call "third order scales").

Measures like Bittner and Goodyear-Grant's are efficient, but they're open to criticisms that they're ignoring the multidimensionality of gender identity by forcing respondents to make a trade-off between masculinity and femininity. However, our work from US samples in recent years shows a very strong negative correlation between scores on a masculinity scale and scores on a femininity scale. That is, even when we give respondents the ability to independently rate their masculinity and femininity, they tend to act as though there's a necessary trade-off between the two: people who give themselves a 90 on femininity give themselves somewhere around a 10 on masculinity, even when no instruction tells them to do so (and even when they're told that they don't have to restrict themselves to 100 points). This tendency was strong enough in the samples we took that there was really no reason to separate out the masculinity and femininity scales, having them both wasn't supplying any information that we weren't getting from a single scale. If a survey was intended for a population in which more diverse gender identities would be expected, or if time spent on a survey wasn't a consideration, two, or more, items would be a good idea, but for a general US population survey with limited space, a single unidimensional gender item seems to work well enough.

Compared to gender, sex may seem like a comparatively simple subject, but measurement of it is similarly fraught. The biological underpinnings of sex categories is much more complex and nuanced than in the lay conception, with many people having a mixture of the traits, like chromosomes, hormones, and reproductive organs, that used to be considered definitively male or female. While standard two-category questions—dividing all respondents into male and female—are fine for most respondents, it may lead researchers to miscategorize some people who don't fall neatly into either camp. That miscategorization is a problem, but having a question that's extra hard for some respondents to answer, or that might make them feel uncomfortable, leads to an even bigger problem for survey research, as those respondents might well choose to hang up on a phone survey or to end an online survey. To the extent that those individuals form a distinct group, our surveys may be missing out on them almost completely, leading to a group that we don't know much about, and that we're missing when we try to understand groups like "registered voters" or "American adults." Thus, while there are certainly moral and theoretical reasons to try to be inclusive with survey questions, there are also logistical reasons: our surveys just aren't going to work very well if we don't include better questions about the sex of respondents.

There is a lot of discussion about the best way to ask survey respondents about their sex. Giving a long list of options may confuse respondents, and also assumes that everyone in a particular SOGI minority group uses the terms offered in the same way, which may not be the case.

Two-step questions, which ask respondents about the sex they were assigned at birth, and the sex they identify with now, do a good job of identifying transgender people, but may lead to a substantial number of false positives, from non-transgender people confused by the questions, from people answering carelessly, or from people who are trolling (a particularly common problem in surveys of teenagers).

Once we adapt measurement techniques to allow for these kinds of differences, we can start to appreciate the complexity of gender identity within sex categories. For instance, using a simple 6-point unidimensional gender identity scale, just 48 percent of men in a 2020 national sample identify as "completely" masculine. Most of the rest say that they're "mostly" masculine, but even that's admitting to some feminine qualities. (See Figure 4.1.)

Only about 5 percent of men place themselves on the feminine side of the spectrum, but almost 10 percent of women say that they're more masculine than feminine. From data like these—and surveys of Canadians have rather similar results, even with a different scale (Bittner and Goodyear-Grant 2017a, 2017b)—we can draw some important conclusions. For most people, sex and gender align, but assuming that questions about sex can serve as a proxy for gender winds up mischaracterizing a substantial minority of respondents who have a gender identity that isn't

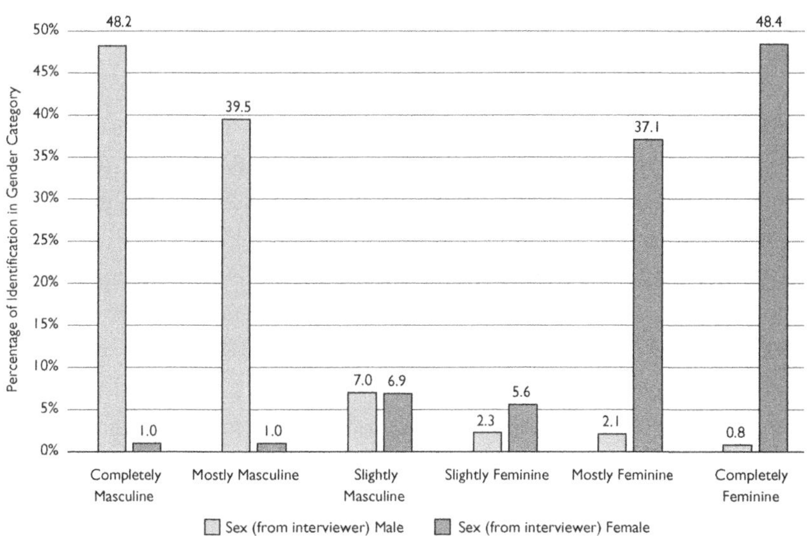

FIGURE 4.1: Stated Gender Identity, by Sex. FDU Poll National Sample.

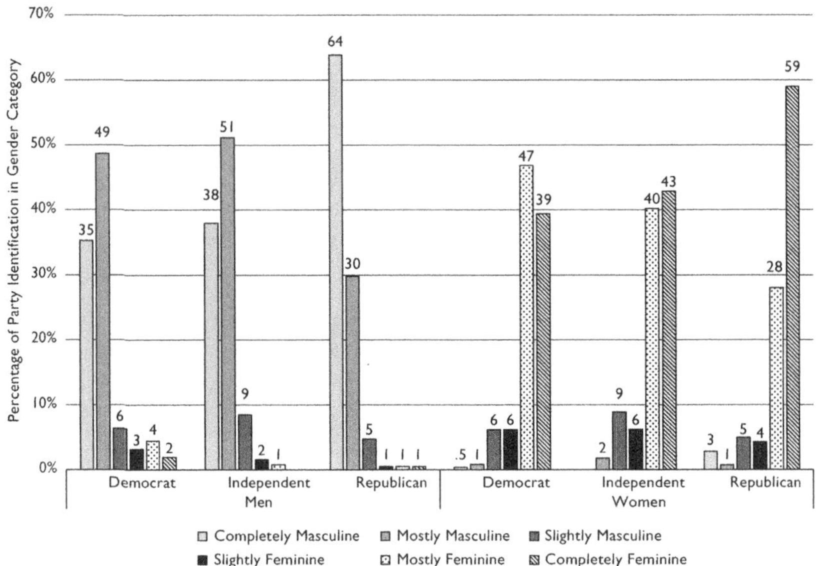

FIGURE 4.2: Stated Gender Identity, by Sex and Party Identification. FDU Poll National Sample.

in line with their sex. Second, there's enormous variation even within those individuals whose sex and gender align. An overwhelming majority of men identify as masculine, but most of them aren't "completely" masculine. This means that measuring gender identity in addition to sex has the potential to tell us a lot about differences even among men who subscribe to gender identities generally in line with their sex.

These differences between men and women are magnified when we look at partisan categories. Just 35 percent of Democratic men identify as "completely" masculine, compared with 64 percent of Republican men. Similarly, Democratic women are much less likely than Republican women to identify as "completely" feminine. (See Figure 4.2.)

It might be tempting to think of the gender divide as being between Republicans who hold traditional gender attitudes—completely masculine men and completely feminine women—and Democrats who don't, but it's not that simple. Republican men have much more traditional gender identities than Republican women do. Women, in general, are more likely than men to say that they have traits associated with men, and Republican women are no exception—about 9 percent of them identify as masculine. Only about 2 percent of Republican men say that they're at all feminine. So, while traditional gender identities are associated with a greater likelihood of identifying as a Republican, something else still seems to be going on with men who identify as being "completely" masculine. Put another way, people with traditional gender identities and men are both more likely to be Republicans and hold conservative political attitudes, but there's an interaction effect, such that men with traditional gender identities are distinct from everyone else.

We can see this difference in party identification, as well as all sorts of other political and social views. On abortion views, for instance, men who identify as completely masculine are significantly less supportive of abortion (higher on the abortion scale in Figure 4.3) than other men and women of any gender identity. In fact, women—both as a single group and in our subgroups—aren't significantly different in their views from men who aren't "completely masculine." On abortion, party identification, gun control measures, hostile sexism scales, and all sorts of other issues, the divide isn't between men and women, but rather between "completely masculine" men and everyone else.

There's also a great deal of variation based on the importance that individuals assign to their gender identity. In the same survey, 42 percent of men say their gender is "extremely" important to their overall conception

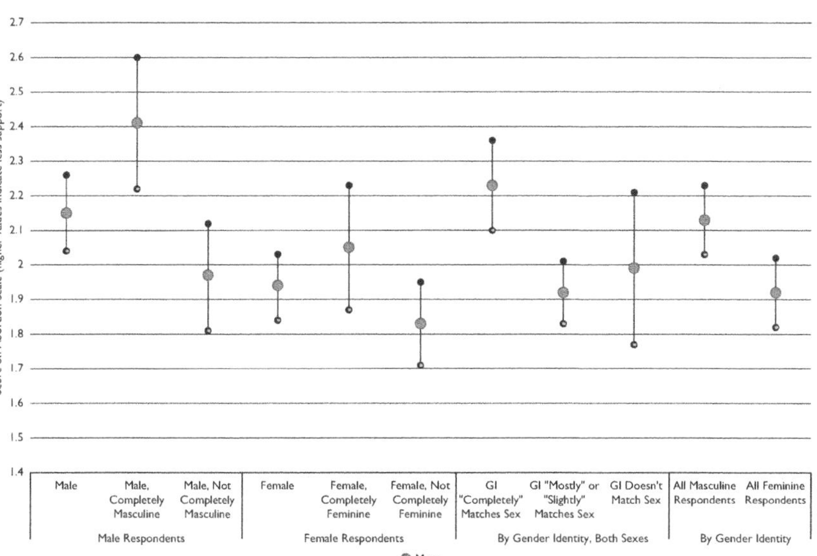

FIGURE 4.3: Abortion Views, by Sex and Gender Identity. FDU Poll National Sample.

of themselves, with 32 percent saying it's "somewhat" important. Among both men and women, people who say hold traditional gender identities are more likely to say that those identities are important to them: 58 percent of men who identify as "completely" masculine say that their gender identity is "extremely" important, compared with 27 percent of other men. Gender identity is least important among those men who identify as being relatively feminine.

The effects of gender identity on men's political views are exaggerated among those men who say that their gender is "extremely" important to them. Among men who say that they're "completely masculine" and that their gender identity is "extremely" important, 48 percent identify as Republican. Among men who identify as "completely masculine" but don't say that their gender identity is "extremely" important, only 27 percent identify as Republican. This makes sense: gender matters more to some people than to others, so it's likely to weigh more heavily in an individual's political and social attitudes when it's more central to that individual's identity (Bittner and Goodyear-Grant 2017a).

Of course, in most of the research discussed in this book, we don't have these kinds of measures of gender identity, and have been looking at the responses of men as a group to find signs of masculinity-based compensatory behaviors. It seems possible that the responses we've seen are driven mostly by men with "completely" masculine gender identities, and perhaps mostly those who also think that their gender identity is very important to their overall identity. As such, figures that look at the responses of men as a whole are likely underestimating the responses of those men, while overestimating the effects on other men.

The linkages between gender identity and political identity are strong enough that, for many men, gender identity and political identity are essentially two ways of expressing the same thing. To look at this, we carried out an online survey in the spring of 2018, in which we experimentally produced a gender identity threat in men by asking them to rate themselves on a set of gender identity scales, bringing up the prospect of a nonbinary conception of gender as a way of inducing threat. Some respondents were randomly assigned to answer questions about their gender identity before answering questions about their partisanship, while other respondents did the opposite. As Monika McDermott (2016) points out, institutions like political parties may be sexless, but that doesn't mean that they're genderless.

When we asked men to rate their gender identity on a set of scales for femininity and masculinity before asking them about their political party, 24 percent of men who said that they were completely masculine, and not at all feminine, said that they were Strong Republicans. But when we asked comparable men about their partisanship first, only 5 percent said that they were Strong Republicans. Similarly, only 10 percent of men who were asked about their gender identity first identified themselves as Strong Democrats; when we asked them about their partisanship first, 38 percent did so. While only about 10 percent of men identify as entirely masculine, and not at all feminine, the same effects pertain, to a lesser degree, to men at all gender identities. It seems that for some men, even raising the possibility that gender identity is a spectrum presents enough of a threat, and is linked enough with partisan politics to push them strongly toward the Republican Party and away from the Democratic Party.

There are no similar effects among female respondents. Identifying as more or less feminine does little to change women's partisan affiliation. But fully understanding these results requires us to delve into the seemingly straightforward concepts of sex and gender.

The gender identity scales that we used ask respondents to place themselves on separate 0 to 100 scales for masculinity and femininity. Because we were worried that respondents would feel that their masculinity or femininity should correspond to their expressed sexual identity (that is, male, female, or one of the other provided options), we also included a set of instructions that normalized non-sex conforming responses, to try to push respondents the other way. These instructions told respondents that gendered traits are societally established, and change over time, so most men have some traits that would be considered feminine, and most women have some traits that would be considered masculine. To further try to normalize non–sex conforming responses, each of the two sliders was initially set to 50, forcing respondents to actively move each of them to get a fully sex-conforming result. The scale and its instructions are shown in Figure 4.4.

In our survey, the median male respondent gave himself an 87 on the masculinity scale, and a 14 on the femininity scale. Even though the instructions tried to push respondents to see masculinity and femininity as not necessarily being in conflict with each other (respondents could, for example give themselves high scores on both or low scores on both), and respondents couldn't see the exact number they were moving each slider

Everyone has a gender identity, which may or may not correspond to physical traits. Rightly or wrongly, society defines certain psychological, emotional or behavioral traits as being masculine and others as being feminine. How these traits are viewed has also shifted enormously over time, so traits that were feminine in the past might be considered masculine today. Because of this, most men have some traits that are considered feminine, and most women have some traits that would be considered masculine. The two traits can co-exist: someone can have feminine qualities and many masculine qualities. How about you? How would place yourself on these scales?

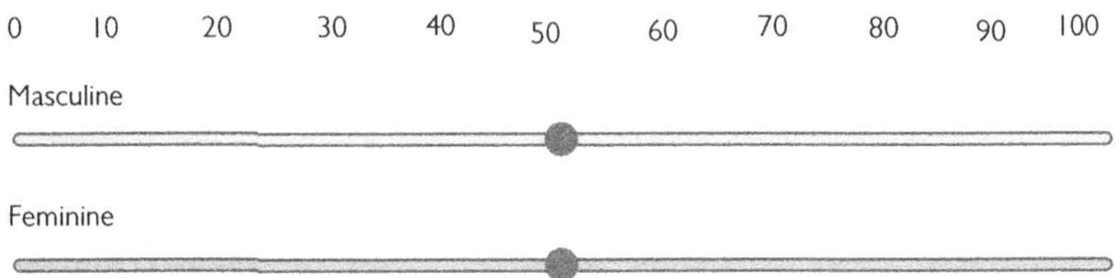

FIGURE 4.4: Gender Identity Scales for Survey.

to, male respondents still got pretty close to complementary responses. Female respondents behaved similarly, but were more willing to admit that they had (socially desirable) masculine traits than men were willing to admit that they had feminine traits. The median female respondent rated herself as a 19 on masculinity and an 82 on femininity.

As noted previously, about 10 percent of men rated themselves at 100 on masculinity and 0 on femininity; only about 5 percent of women rated themselves at 100 on femininity and 0 on masculinity. Because the masculinity scores respondents assigned to themselves were so tightly correlated, we were able to combine them into a single score by subtracting the adherence to the gender not aligned with a respondent's chosen sex from the adherence to the gender that was aligned with his or her sex. So, a woman who placed herself at 85 on the femininity scale and 10 on the masculinity scale would score a 75. To the extent that masculinity and femininity aren't necessarily in tension with one another, such a score could misrepresent the gender identities of some respondents; but because our respondents treated masculinity and femininity as if they were in tension, this scoring worked as a reasonable way to summarize the responses into one measure, as shown in Figure 4.5.

We should note that this is one of the areas in which we reach a conclusion different from McDermott's analysis of gender identity, which uses the BSRI, as discussed previously. Perhaps because items on the BSRI assess gender indirectly (through traits rather than asking directly),

McDermott finds that US men are more feminine than US women are masculine, though this result could also be due to differences in sampling. In addition, she had a relatively large proportion of respondents who were either high or low in both masculine traits and feminine traits, something we don't see in any of our data sets. This goes to show how important questions about measurement in this area really are.

While 100 is the modal score on our combined scale (corresponding to a score of 100 on the gender that aligns with the respondent's chosen sex and 0 on the other gender), it still represents only about 10 percent of the respondents, with the median respondent scoring an 85. While they may view masculinity and femininity as being part of a trade-off, most of our respondents are perfectly comfortable claiming a gender identity that's somewhat masculine and somewhat feminine.

As discussed previously, when men answer these gender identity items prior to answering the question about their political party, they tend to align the responses. Men who rate themselves as more masculine become more likely to say they're Republicans, and less likely to say they're Democrats. Men who rate themselves as less masculine become more likely to say they're Democrats, and less likely to say they're Republicans.

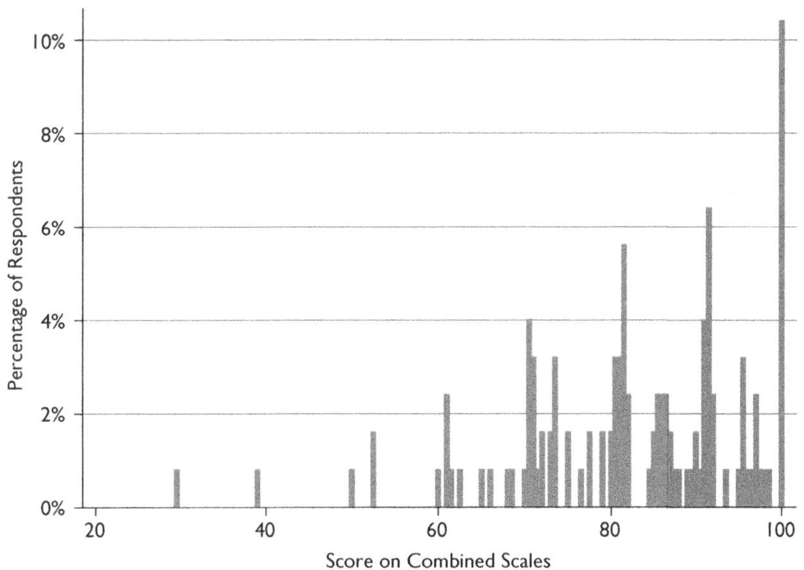

FIGURE 4.5: Scores on Combined Masculine Scale and Feminine Scale.

To understand why the issue of gender identity might be moving the way in which people express their partisanship, we have to have some understanding of what partisanship is. In general, political scientists debate over two main models of partisanship (as described by Leonie Huddy and Alexa Bankert 2017). One camp holds that partisanship is primarily instrumental, a summary of what the individual believes, which may not be entirely identical to what the perceived current leaders of the party are thought to believe. In this view, individuals are thought to be rational when picking a party, and a party that moves too much will lose their support. Expressive partisanship, in contrast, holds that political party is a social identity like any other, reinforced by overlap with other social identities, like gender, race, and religion. The difference is important: if people are instrumental partisans, they'll be focused on policy outcomes, and be willing to compromise with the other side to achieve them. If they're expressive partisans, policy may be almost entirely beside the point, as partisans seek to win, or deny the other side a win, whether it achieves anything or not.

At this point in US politics, the expressive partisanship side seems, on the evidence, to have a clear advantage, even if some voters (especially those with high levels of political information) may be pragmatic enough to be considered instrumentalists. These results fit right in with this narrative: priming respondents to think about their gender identity makes that identity more salient in their decision about which political identity to claim. The respondents in our sample seem to have decided at some point that masculinity is linked with the Republican Party, and femininity—or at least a rejection of masculinity—is linked with the Democratic Party. By making those gender identities more relevant, we're, at least temporarily, strengthening the importance of that link, pushing men to align their partisanship and gender.

Bittner and Goodyear-Grant (2017a) argue that because the salience of gender isn't equally distributed throughout the population, one shouldn't expect the effects of gender identity on behavior to be equally distributed either. We described an example of this in Chapter 3: when the sex of a candidate is stressed, men become more likely to oppose female candidates. Putting the sex of a candidate front and center tends to make gender more salient, making it more likely that men will make decisions on the basis of their own gender identity. Similarly, the measures of sexism we've used may well be thought of as measures of the overall salience of gender to men's social and political beliefs: men who are high in sexism measures may just be more likely to apply a gender lens to any issue they see. We may not have a direct measure of sexism embedded in the surveys discussed in this chapter, but we know from other studies that Republican men, in general, have higher levels of sexism than Democratic men. As such, they may perceive a greater link between their partisanship and their gender identity. This also leads to an alternate reading of the findings here: without a control group, a third political party that doesn't exist in the United States, we can't distinguish between masculinity making men more Republican and a rejection of masculinity making men more Democratic. It's possible that what we're seeing is one-sided, with masculinity linked with Republican partisanship, and simply the absence of an effect on the other side. But, as with cash discounts and credit card surcharges at gas stations, whether an effect is increasing on one side or decreasing on the other, the net effect is exactly the same.

But if partisanship and gender are being aligned, the relationship should go both ways. That is, if making men think about their gender identity makes them more likely to identify with the party that they feel matches that identity, asking them about their party should shift their expression of their gender identity. We can use the same experimental set-up to test this relationship, and see whether men get more or less masculine men after they identify themselves as Republicans or Democrats.

This shift is exactly what happened. Men in the political identity first condition gave themselves lower scores on the combined scale as their party identification became more Democratic. So on the one hand, men who rated themselves as Strong Republicans (about 9% of men) have an expected combined scale score of 95 in the experimental condition—but a score of only 83 in the gender identity first condition (in which they responded to the femininity and masculinity scales before the political scales). On the other hand, men who identified as Strong Democrats had an expected combined score value of 76 in the experimental condition—and 85 in the control condition. Essentially, there is no relationship between expressed partisanship and combined scale scores in the gender identity first condition, and a substantial effect in the political identity first condition. (See Figures 4.6 and 4.7.)

This effect does not hold for women. Among men in the experimental condition, a 1-point increase in party identification is expected to lead to a 4-point decrease in the masculinity-femininity combined score. For

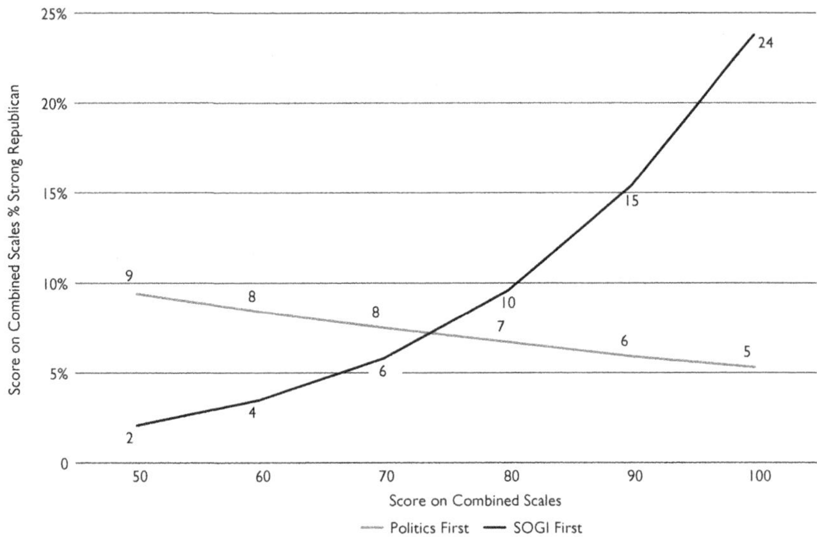

FIGURE 4.6: Expected Percentage Strong Republican, by Condition and Score on Combined Scale, for Men.

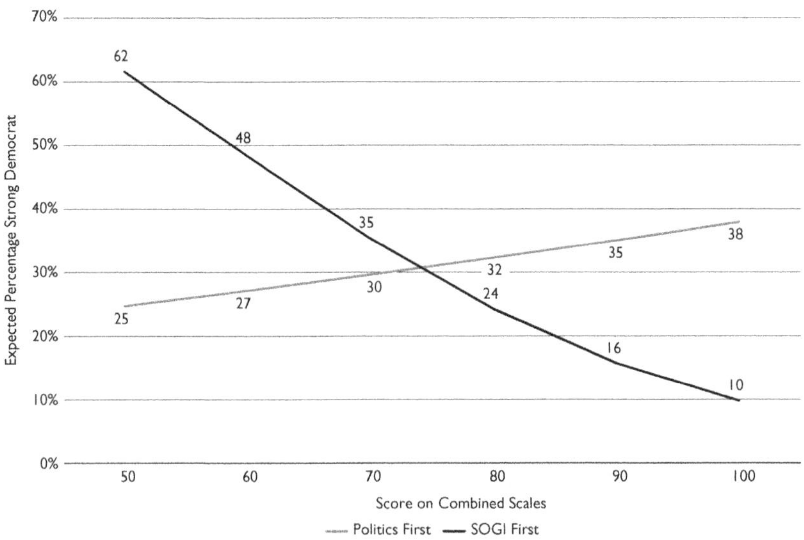

FIGURE 4.7: Expected Percentage Strong Democrat, by Condition and Score on Combined Scale, for Men.

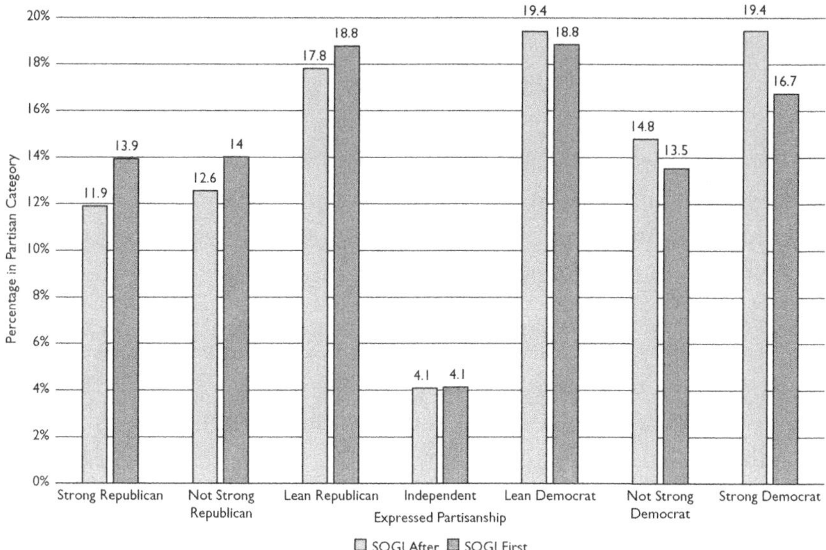

FIGURE 4.8: Expected Party Identification, by Condition. Source: Data from TESS.

women in the experimental condition, the effect is less than 1 point, and in the opposite direction (but not statistically significant). (See Figure 4.8.)

If these effects are working the way that they seem to be, with expressions of sexual and gender identity driving expressions of partisanship, they shouldn't be produced only by the gender scales that we've been using in these studies. Indeed, any question that primes respondents to think about their gender identity should have similar effects.

To see if this holds up, we make use of an unintentional experiment from a large-scale survey carried out in late 2015 and early 2016. The survey was an omnibus, containing sets of questions from many different researchers, put together in a random order. One of those research teams consisted of Laurel Westbrook of Grand Valley State University and Aliya Saperstein of Stanford University, who were testing a new technique for identifying transgender individuals in surveys (Westbrook and Saperstein 2015). Rather than using a single item asking if respondents are transgender, they used several questions, first asking respondents about their assigned sex at birth, and then asking about their current sex. To avoid false positives resulting from rushed answers or misunderstandings, Westbrook and Saperstein added a third question, asking the respondents who had identified as having different sexes currently and at birth if they were, indeed, transgender. Because of the randomization, half of the respondents were asked about their partisanship—using the same 7-point party scales used elsewhere—before being asked whether they were transgender, and half were asked about party afterward. Among those asked about party after being asked if they were transgender, about half were asked immediately afterward, and half received other unrelated questions in between. (See the Methodology Notes for full details of the analyses in this chapter.)

While the effects are relatively smaller than in the previous experiment, the manipulation is also likely less threatening. After all, the questions were basic enough that respondents might not have even realized that they were being asked about transgender status. Even so, asking the items first increased the number of Republicans in the sample by 5 points, and decreased the number of Democrats by just a bit less than that. Unlike the outcome in some other analyses, we don't see a polarization effect here, in which respondents with some preexisting characteristics become more Democratic, but perhaps that's because the questions activated gender identity for only some respondents.

Still, the results are in line with what we've seen in the other analyses. Making respondents think about their gender identity or sexuality changes the way that they think about their political identities, telling us that they see a connection between the two. For respondents in the United States, Republicanism and masculinity are linked, and expressions of masculinity, or of cisgender identity, lead respondents to be more likely to identify as Republicans.

It would be nice if we could also replicate the other side of the first study, showing that asking about political identity first impacts the ways in which respondents answer the two-step transgender items. The transgender items, unlike the gender scales we used earlier, are dichotomous: a certain sex assigned at birth and a certain sex now. There's no gray area, and while it's possible that respondents who answered the political items first responded differently, there aren't enough transgender individuals in the data set for us to be sure.

The study respondents discussed here seem to think there's a link between gender, sexuality, and political views—but is there? In her review of the research, Ewa A. Golebiowska (2019), of Wayne State University, finds that beliefs about gender roles and sexuality have immediate effects on preferred policies, especially with regard to issues touching on sexuality. However, partisanship isn't the best predictor of views of SOGI minorities. That predictor, she finds, is contact: having a close friend or relative who belongs to a SOGI group makes someone much more likely to support the group. Religion and moral traditionalism matter as well, but ideas about gender roles are part of it: individuals with less flexible conceptions of gender roles are much more likely to oppose rights for members of SOGI minority groups. Of course, identification with a SOGI minority shapes political and social views as well: members of SOGI minority groups tend be more liberal, and more Democratic, than similarly situated individuals who aren't part of those groups. They also favor protections for minority groups of all stripes, though self-identified bisexuals are a little less likely to do so.

We can use the 2018 AP VoteCast survey of a large number of registered voters, large enough to have a substantial sample of individuals from SOGI minority groups, to see how self-identified lesbian, gay, and bisexual respondents are different from heterosexuals. While they're generally more liberal than heterosexuals—less than 10 percent of LGB respondents are "somewhat" or "very" conservative, compared to 32 percent of heterosexuals—once we control for party, the differences are muted. Essentially, LGB individuals are more likely to be Democrats, but LGB Democrats and heterosexual Democrats have very similar views on most issues. For instance, on a scale measuring support for Trump, LGB Democrats had a mean score of 3.7; heterosexual Democrats had a mean score of 3.8. The only area of significant difference within parties is on abortion rights, where LGB-identifying Democrats are markedly more in favor of abortion rights than heterosexual Democrats. LGB-identifying Republicans don't seem much different from heterosexual Republicans, but there aren't enough LGB Republicans, even in the huge VoteCast sample, to be sure.

So, while partisanship may not be the best predictor of views of homosexuals, there does seem to be a link between beliefs about gender identities and policy views, as well as between sexuality and partisanship. Respondents who have just identified themselves as Republicans might rationally decide that they must also hold more traditional gender roles, because Republicans, in general, do. The relationship between their own gender identity and their partisanship may be all in their heads, but they're not necessarily wrong.

In addition to priming the perceived relationship between partisanship and gender identity, questions about sexuality can serve as threats, leading men to adopt compensatory behaviors, as described throughout this book. To see how this might work, we can go back to the VoteCast survey. In an effort to save respondents' time on the lengthy survey, most respondents were randomly assigned to one of four different forms, each of which had some shared, and some unique questions. This meant that about one in four respondents got two questions, almost at the tail end of the survey—one asking respondents if they were "gay, lesbian or bisexual," and the other asking if they were "transgender," allowing us to see how men react to being explicitly asked if they are homosexual. Placing certain questions at the end like this is standard practice in surveys, as researchers want to give the interviewer as much time as possible to build rapport with respondents, so they'll be more willing to answer. If respondents aren't willing to answer and just hang up, having such questions at the end of the survey means that at least not much other information is lost.

Immediately after the LGBT items on the survey was another question—which was posed to all the respondents—asking them whether or not they owned a gun. Overall, 42.9 percent of respondents said that they did (because this survey was designed as an exit poll equivalent, rather than an overall population sample, these figures may not correspond to actual gun ownership rates in the United States). When men hadn't been asked about their sexuality, 46.2 percent of them said that they had a gun in their household: 41 percent said that they themselves owned a gun, and another 5 percent said that someone else in their household had one. But when men were asked about their LGBT status, the number who claimed to have a gun in their household jumped from 46.2 percent to 49.4 percent, with nearly all of the gain coming from claims that they, personally, owned the gun. (See Figure 4.9.) Essentially, asking men if they're gay leads to 4 percent of them suddenly deciding they have guns that they otherwise would not have had.

We're not the first to find a similar effect. Political psychologist Karen Stenner (2005) carried out a study in which teams of two survey researchers were sent to conduct face-to-face interviews. The second interviewer on each team was randomly assigned, and respondents whose households had been randomly assigned a second interviewer who was African-American became much more likely to tell the interviewers that

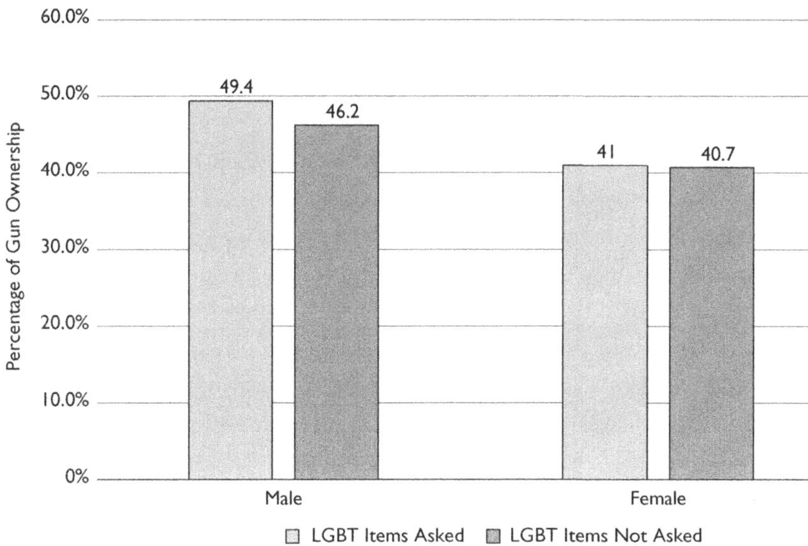

FIGURE 4.9: Percentage Reporting Gun Ownership, by Sex, if LGBT Items Asked

there was a gun in the house. Note that this wasn't in response to a question about gun ownership—the respondents were doing it spontaneously, apparently in response to the seeming threat posed by the silent African-American interviewer. We explore the link between firearms and masculinity with greater depth in a later chapter, but the point here is that threat is easily raised, so just asking about sexuality, as the AP VoteCast survey did, is itself considered a threat that merits a compensatory response.

Still, there's at least a theoretical distinction to be made between these compensatory behaviors and the perceived link between gender identity and partisanship. Among men in the United States, being Republican is part of being straight and being masculine, just as having even a slightly less traditional gender identity is part of being a Democrat. These views may well be based on reality—after all, people with the most traditional gender identities are more likely to be Republicans—but the survey results show exactly how closely linked these identities are in men's minds. This link is distinct from the potential threat that arises from asking questions about men's sexuality or gender identity: as the last analysis shows, even attempts to gauge men's sexuality can be interpreted as a threat, leading them to adopt compensatory behaviors. Like our political identities, our sexual and gender identities are a big part of how we present ourselves to the world, and how we understand our own place in it. There's no necessary relationship between heterosexuality and Republicanism or between femininity and being a Democrat, but such identities have become intrinsically linked.

So, why did the issue of transgender access to bathrooms become so fraught, so quickly? It doesn't seem that it had to be this way: after all, Republicans have long argued for local control and for keeping the government out of the decisions of private individuals and businesses, so there's an alternate world in which Republican-controlled legislatures let local school boards and businesses decide for themselves how, or whether, to regulate access to restrooms. But, instead, many of them passed laws overriding local control on these issues and regulating access within businesses. This wasn't even a divisive issue among Republicans: because, it seems, gender identity and sexual orientation are built into political identity. This is all without bringing in the potential threat arising from recognition of alternate sexual and gender identities, which might itself lead to more conservative issue positions as compensatory responses.

Of course, the news isn't all bad for proponents of the rights of SOGI minorities. There is diversity of gender and sexual identity among men in the United States, and we've seen some signs of the sort of polarization that's most evident in political questions. Nevertheless, an enormous transformation in public attitudes toward homosexuals in the United States has occurred over the past 20 years, largely driven by a positive reinforcement cycle in which homosexuality is more accepted, so more individuals are willing to identify themselves to friends and family. This leads to greater acceptance, and more individuals identifying themselves. It's possible we could see a similar cycle arise with other SOGI minority groups, perhaps eventually disconnecting the issue of gender and sexual identity from partisan politics altogether.

CHAPTER 5

GOD, GUNS, AND PORNOGRAPHY

Up to this point, we have taken our general framework of examining how men react to threats to their gender identities and applied it to various places in men's lives. But the understanding of gender threat that we are developing here is not limited to the areas we've discussed so far. It can be applied to all sorts of behaviors that aren't as obviously linked to masculinity as political behaviors, or sexual harassment in the workplace. Gender permeates every aspect of our lives, so almost any behavior, if some men associate it with an important aspect of masculinity, can become a way for men to express their gender identities. These activities can then become a way for men to reinforce that masculinity when it's threatened by the loss, or the potential loss, of an important part of their understanding of what it means to be a man.

In this chapter, we focus on three areas in which men in the United States are responding to masculinity threats by doubling down on a behavior not directly linked to the existence of the threat: religion, gun ownership, and use of pornography. These particular issues are, of course, also important in American politics. Religion, gun ownership, and pornography all have a history of being important issues in American elections. We'll explain how each behavior has become linked to masculinity, and demonstrate how men change their activities or attitudes in that area when their masculinity is threatened. While we've tried to present examples that are socially relevant in the United States at this time, we also

believe that these instances are just the tip of the iceberg. Gender identity is enormously important to men, and they're nothing if not creative in coming up with ways to assert their masculinity.

RELIGION

An outsize share of the research on masculinity and religion has focused on a men's revival movement known as the Promise Keepers. The Promise Keepers are an evangelical Christian organization, founded in 1990 by the then head football coach at the University of Colorado Boulder. The organization posits that men are essentially aggressive, sinful creatures, yet they can rise above their base natures by following the perceived example of Jesus as a compassionate, caring leader. The group's ministry argues that men have a responsibility to be in charge of their households, communities, and churches, and blames the problems of modern American society on the failure of men to overcome their "natural tendencies" or their failure to take command once they have succeeded in reforming themselves. The group spent some years as a rising force in mainstream US evangelical circles, peaking at a 1997 event on the National Mall that attracted more than half a million attendees, and it has attracted praise and financial support from evangelical leaders like James Dobson and Pat Robertson.

The Promise Keepers movement has been linked closely with gender research because it is explicitly based on appeals to masculinity. Even today, the overview of the group's beliefs on the Promise Keepers website starts by proclaiming "Masculinity is in crisis," and explaining that "men long for respect, purpose, and influence in their homes and communities, among their friends, and in the workplace." However, it continues, men don't know how to achieve these goals, leading them to depression and to addictions to pornography, alcohol, and drugs. The pitch is clearly aimed at men who have failed to meet the expectations of hegemonic masculinity, and it is offering them an alternate path to achieving those expectations.

Melanie Heath, a sociologist at McMaster University in Ontario, conducted an ethnography with members of the Promise Keepers movement and their wives to look at how men in the movement used the religion to bolster their masculine identities (Heath 2003). While the men at the Promise Keepers' rallies talked about how great it was that they could hold hands and cry and hug other men without anyone thinking it was "funny" (which, in context, seems to mean "gay"), it was also important to them that women were not welcome at these events, as both the men and their wives said that men can't be comfortable with these behaviors if women are present. It also helped that the rallies were held in sports stadiums, so that the men could accompany their religious practice with the trappings of more traditional masculinity: team jerseys and hats, shouted slogans, and the like. One of the major themes of these rallies has been the need for men to care less about money and being primary breadwinners, and care more about being parents, husbands, and leaders in their churches and communities. Of course, this doesn't sound like a bad thing, given that Americans spend more time at work than people in most other industrialized nations, but it also gives men in the group a way to reinforce their masculine identity without being a breadwinner. For them, being a good father and husband makes them *more* of a man than someone who mainly just earns money.

This focus on finding different ways to be a "good man" extends into marital relations as well. Heath's participants spoke a great deal about relations between men and their wives, with both men and women voicing the view that men had to be the final decision makers in a household. There should be discussions, and a man should take his wife's views into account, but at the end of the day, he makes the final decision (even when the couple being interviewed couldn't think of any particular instances where he had actually done so). Having the final say is an important part of how these men construct their masculine identities, reinforcing the idea that they are in charge, at least symbolically, whether they're the breadwinners in their households or not.

It doesn't seem to be a coincidence that members of the Promise Keepers are dominantly middle- and upper-class white men (though the movement has pushed racial reconciliation as an important aspect of its ministry, and appointed a number of men of color to leadership positions), a demographic that was, and remains, politically conservative. Of course, the ministries promoted by groups like the Promise Keepers aren't limited to masculinity issues. Other researchers, like Newton (2005), have looked at other aspects of the Promise Keepers' ministry, and found some reason for optimism in members' views on race relations and compassion for their wives. But the overall story should seem familiar at this point: men who are unable to live up to the standards they believe society has set for them in one area compensate by doubling down in another area.

In this case, Promise Keepers is telling men not only that they don't need to earn a lot of money but also that a focus on earning money is at odds with what men should be doing. Rather than being breadwinners, they should focus on being leaders in their church or their community. Even if they don't have decision-making authority on household spending or vacations, they can have what amounts to a completely symbolic "final say" that they may never actually use.

On the one hand, given what we know about how some men in society in general behave toward their wives and families when they feel that they aren't meeting the standards of hegemonic masculinity, reports that Promise Keeper men wind up with better relationships make sense. As the ministry gives them symbolic and spiritual authority, they don't need to assert their masculinity in other ways that might be more harmful to their relationships. On the other hand, Michael Messner (1997) describes the Promise Keepers, as a whole, as being part of a "politicized anti-feminist and anti-gay backlash" against increasing equality in society. The members may talk about being more caring as husbands, but they do so with the purpose of having greater control over their wives and children. The underlying message isn't about rejecting traditional masculinities: it's about achieving them via religious means when other routes have been blocked off.

These views of the men's proper role in a marriage and in society are perhaps most clearly explicated among the Promise Keepers, but the American evangelical movement more generally pushes very similar views. Evangelical sects believe in ontological differences between men and women (Burke and Hudec 2015), arguing a man is called to follow God, while a woman's true role is to support the leadership of her husband and of the other men leading her church, community, and nation. As the statement of beliefs of the Southern Baptist Convention puts it: "A husband . . . has the God-given responsibility to provide for, to protect, and to lead his family. A wife is to submit herself graciously to the servant [of Christ] leadership of her husband." There are, of course, plenty of examples of female leadership in Christian traditions, some of which have been embraced by reform-minded churches. So why the focus here on male dominance and female submission? We argue that it is giving men a way to respond to challenges to male dominance in society. As with so many of the other behaviors discussed in this book, some men use an association with evangelical religion as a way to bolster an otherwise threatened masculine identity.

This may be most evident in edge cases. For instance, J. E. Sumerau, a sociologist at the University of Tampa, looked at how gay Christian men use religion to define their masculine identities (Sumerau 2012). The men in their study define masculinity, in part, through fatherhood, but as this is largely denied to them, they focus instead on roles as spiritual leaders, taking charge of their communities, guiding gay men who have recently come out, and stressing the inherent rationality of men. As one of their participants put it, “I think sometimes the drama gets the best of women, but it’s not their fault, they’re not built like us, and that’s just how it is. Men just seem to know how to handle the important stuff.” The belief in inherent differences between men and women seems to be uniquely valuable to men needing to assert their gender identities in the face of decreasing male privilege: to the extent that men are different, and better, ontologically, their status can never really be challenged.

While men from conservative religious sects may talk about the importance of taking care of their families, there’s little evidence that they actually put more work into those families. Indeed, studies that have looked at what they actually do (especially with regard to childcare and messy tasks like feeding and diaper changes) show that they do less relative to their wives than men from other sects, or those who have no religion at all, do (DeMaris, Mahoney, and Pargament 2011). The biggest study of the question (Civettini and Glass 2008) finds that men from conservative religious backgrounds don’t get married earlier, have children earlier, or work different hours than similarly situated men from other denominations. This is especially jarring given that women from the same conservative religious backgrounds *do* get married earlier than other women. The claims being made by members of these sects seem to be largely symbolic.

These sorts of conservative, traditionalist, and evangelical Christian traditions provide men with a way to assert their masculinity when they believe that they’ve fallen short in some other way. As such, it should be the case that inducing some degree of threat in men will lead them to be more likely to identity with these religious beliefs. To examine how this works, we looked at what led American men to claim a “born-again” or “evangelical” identity in a massive poll at the time of the 2018 US midterm election.

When collecting the data used in its enormous exit poll replacement, AP VoteCast, the Associated Press had a number of questions that were state or region specific, as well as some that had been cut from the basic survey owing to time constraints (an over-long survey is a very bad thing). Because of this, the AP divided up many of the questions in its survey into four question forms, with each respondent being randomly assigned to one of the forms, as well as any items designed specifically for their state (only respondents from Tennessee were asked about approval of Taylor Swift, for instance). In addition, the AP randomly assigned some respondents to get extra questions from one of the other forms. This was a relatively small portion of the sample, but in a survey as big as the AP VoteCast, which had a sample size of more than 138,000, even a small portion is more responses than most surveys ever collect.

The fact that groups of respondents were randomly assigned to different sets of questions amounted to a survey experiment, even if that was not a purpose for the VoteCast team. We took advantage of this experiment to look at the effects of asking questions about gender relations and sexual orientation on how men described their religious beliefs. One form of the survey included two items about the #MeToo movement (asking how concerned respondents were about women's allegations not being believed, and about men not being given the opportunity to defend themselves against allegations) and also items asking respondents if they were gay, lesbian, bisexual, or transgender. After getting these questions—and almost immediately after the question about LGBT status—respondents were asked about their religious views: what denomination they affiliated with, and whether they considered themselves to be a born-again or evangelical Christian.

In the previous chapter, we showed that bringing up gender identity can lead men to feel that their gender identity is being threatened, leading them to then adopt compensatory attitudes or behaviors. We should note that because the #Metoo and LGBT items were always asked together on the VoteCast survey, we have no way of figuring out which one was causing the threat, but for our purposes, it hardly matters: the question is the extent to which men responded to these potentially threatening questions by changing their reported religious views. We made use of a logistic regression analysis to isolate this effect. (See the Methodology Notes for details of this chapter's analyses relating to religion, gun ownership, and use of pornography.)

Overall, 25 percent of men (and 30 percent of women) described themselves as being born again or evangelical. Twenty percent of men who described themselves as "very liberal" said that they were born again or evangelical, but that dropped to 16 percent among those who were asked the potentially threatening questions. Among "very conservative" men, however, the threatening items *increased* the likelihood that they would identify as being born again or evangelical, from 40 percent among those who weren't asked, to 52 percent of those who were. As with many of the political issues, gender role threat leads men to polarize: in this case, conservative men are more likely to claim that they have a more traditionalist set of religious views, while liberal men move the opposite direction. (See Figure 5.1.)

This seeming polarization highlights another recurring finding: gender threat has very different effects on conservative and liberal men. Defining masculinity differently in the first place necessarily means changing what it means to double down on that masculine identity. Liberal men who might otherwise identify as evangelical, seem to, in the face of threat, move away from that inherently gendered identification. Conservative men, looking to strengthen an assertion of a masculine identity, move toward it.

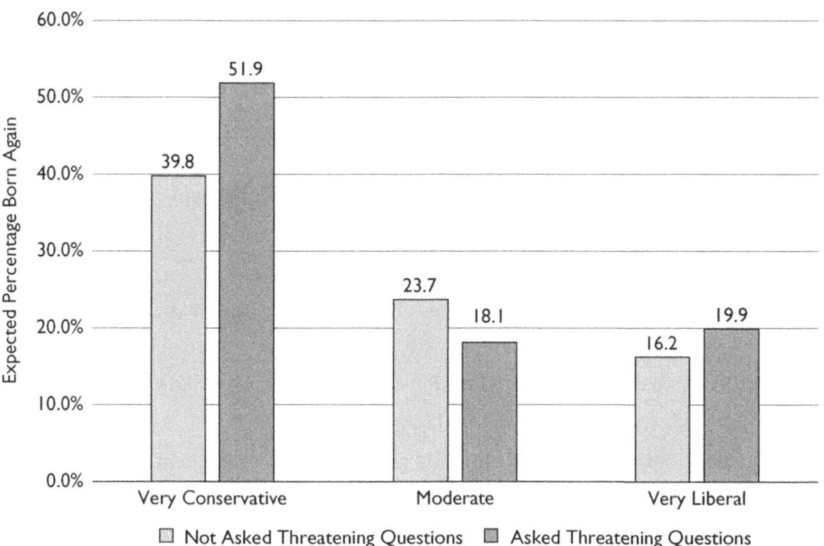

FIGURE 5.1: Percentage of Men Saying They Are Born Again, by Condition and Ideology.

Like most of the compensatory behaviors we've discussed, these behaviors are likely shaped by men's social environments. Asserting masculinity through a born-again or evangelical identification is going to work best in places and times where that identification is recognized as a source of masculine power. In essence, these sorts of religious compensatory activities are likely to be centered in areas where there are already lots of evangelical or born-again Christians, individuals to whom the claiming of a certain religious identity would be meaningful.

Such results also help to establish the role that identifying as born again holds in reinforcing men's gender identities. When men face threat, from questions asking about their sexuality or questions that bring up the #MeToo movement, they become more likely to say that they're born again. This is a survey experiment, so there's no chance that the threat has changed the churches men go to in the time since the threatening items were asked. So, the results are telling us that these men view being born again as a meaningful response to the threat. It doesn't matter that they may not actually go to church: claiming to be part of a religious movement that stresses male dominance is enough to alleviate some of the strain created by the gender threat.

GUNS

Like religion, gun ownership plays a central role in modern American politics. In the United States, 42 percent of people have a firearm in their home, and firearms have played an important role in the construction of masculinity (Stroud 2012; Stange and Oyster 2000; Melzer 2012), Like religion, gun ownership provides a way for men to bolster a threatened gender identity. Of course, we don't think that men are likely to admit that guns are being used to make up for some failure to conform to an idealized masculine identity, but by parsing the data carefully, we can show that gender role threat is playing a major role in driving gun sales in the United States. To put it simply, when men come under threat, they buy more guns. The more prevalent guns are in their locale, they more they do it. Many of the compensatory behaviors that we've discussed have social implications but are still largely personal, impacting mostly men and their families. Gun purchases, however, are closer in their effects to changes in political views: both of these may be decisions driven by men's psyches, but they have consequences for the rest of the society. During the Great Recession, millions of married men became unemployed while their wives did not: our analysis indicates that during this period, this difference in unemployment rates led to about 1.1 million additional background checks, representing the sale of at least that many guns. The crisis of gun violence in our country is, to an extent, a crisis of masculinity.

Of course, "supporting my gender identity" doesn't come up much when men are asked why they own a gun. The most common reason American gun owners cite for owning a firearm is protection, but this explanation doesn't seem to hold up when we look at the data. In the late 1990s, when the Federal Bureau of Investigation started collecting information on gun sales in the United States, as part of the National Instant Criminal Background Check System (NICS), there were about 600,000 individual gun purchases through licensed dealers per month. By 2018, that figure had grown to more than 2 million per month. Over that same period, violent crime in the United States dropped by more than a quarter, from 523 crimes per hundred thousand residents to 383. If gun ownership is about protection from criminals, we would expect gun sales to would have gone down along with crime rates over the years, rather than increasing. It's possible that these gun owners—who are overwhelmingly male (Carroll 2005)—are responding to the fear of crime, or images of crime on television, rather than actual crime rates. But while there may be something to the idea that men have overblown fears of victimization, such an explanation ignores the ways in which guns play into traditional images of masculinity.

It seems almost Freudian to argue for a link between men's gender identities and guns, but that link is now well established in the sociological literature. We've already talked about the masculine ideals of being a family man and a protector of the household and the community, and owning a gun can allow men to feel they are better fulfilling these roles. University of Arizona sociologist Jennifer Carlson (2015) has used a qualitative study of male gun carriers in Michigan to explore the symbolic dimensions of gun ownership for men. In the imagination of gun owners, having a firearm may allow them to better shield vulnerable wives and children, and carrying a concealed weapon means that they might be able to be the "good guy with a gun" who protects the community from criminal violence. This potential violence, in Carlson's work, is highly raced and classed: the "bad guys" are generally envisioned as racial or ethnic minorities, and the racist tropes inherent in protecting white women from these interlopers are clear. For most men, the role of protector may not be the most important element of a masculine gender identity: roles such as provider and father may generally be more dominant, but when men perceive that they aren't meeting one aspect of their role as men, we've seen how they can double down on what might otherwise be a less important aspect.

This link between gender and guns is evident from survey data on the topic. As noted in Chapter 4, men in the AP VoteCast survey who were randomly assigned to be asked whether or not they were homosexual were more likely to say that they owned a gun than those men who weren't asked about their sexuality.

We can deepen our understanding through other survey work. A survey taken in the run-up to the 2018 Congressional midterm election in the United States asked Americans about gun control, and separately, measured their views on traditional gender relations using a hostile sexism scale. Overall, on a 5-point scale asking about desired changes to the availability of guns in the United States, 38 percent of Americans put themselves on the lowest end of the scale, saying that it should be *more* difficult to buy all kinds of guns, and 13 percent put themselves in the highest two categories, saying that it should be *easier* to buy guns (8 percent were in the highest category). After controlling for partisanship, age, education, and employment status, 23 percent of men holding the most traditional gender views said that it should be easier to buy guns. Only 7 percent of men with the least traditional gender views said the same.

How big is the effect of views of gender? Being a strong Democrat, instead of a strong Republican, makes men 28 points more likely to support restrictions on gun sales. Being at the highest level of the hostile sexism scale—essentially asserting the necessary dominance of men over women—rather than at the low end of the scale makes men 30 points less likely to support restrictions on gun sales. So, how much does a man's view of gender roles impact his views of firearms? About as much as his political party does. (See Figure 5.2.)

To some extent, exploiting the link between masculinity and guns has been a strategy on the part of gun advocacy groups. Sociologists like Scott Melzer and Kevin Lewis O'Neill have examined how gun lobby groups, and especially the National Rifle Association, have made use of appeals to masculinity in marketing gun ownership. Scott Melzer (2012) has looked at how the narratives used in NRA materials link gun ownership to what he calls "frontier masculinity," the idea that men cannot depend on the

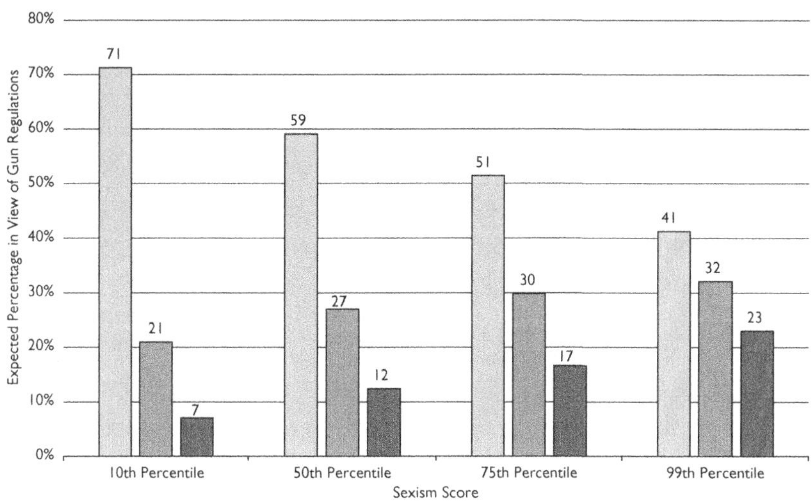

FIGURE 5.2: Expected Views of Gun Control.
SOURCE: Data from DPF.

government to protect families from threats that inevitably arise. As such, guns are seen to be part of self-reliance and a strong work ethic. Not having a gun means that you're dependent on the state, which might be unreliable or incompetent, or even on the side of the groups that are threatening you. In recent years, as the NRA has become more politicized, this view of masculinity seems to have led the group to take public stances on issues that don't seem to have anything to do with guns, just with masculinity itself, like affirmative action and government assistance to the needy. If the government is trustworthy and competent, there's less need for individuals to own a gun; but if the government is thought of as corrupt or in the pocket of the forces perceived to be aligned against middle-class white men, a gun is the only way to take care of yourself and your family. This also helps to explain the resistance to popular, and seemingly commonsense, proposals like expanding background checks, or placing limits on firearm purchases by the mentally ill: guns are seen as nothing less than freedom from government dependency.

O'Neill's work on NRA narratives focuses on the stories in the NRA's flagship magazine, *The American Rifleman*, and "The Armed Citizen" section in particular (O'Neill 2007). The stories in this section are classic "good guy with a gun" narratives, in which individuals use firearms to defend themselves and their families from criminals. What's interesting about these stories, as O'Neill points out, is the frequency with which the individuals using a gun are physically disabled, or elderly, or sick. But since they have a gun, they're not vulnerable, and are able to use the gun to take on a traditionally masculine role—even when they're women—by protecting themselves and their families. Of course, instances of people using firearms defensively are rare, but by highlighting the possibility, and building narratives around such individuals, these stories make the reader think there's an epidemic of violence threatening their families that can be stopped only by guns and a willingness to use them. When men say that they're getting a gun in order to protect themselves and their families, they're not lying: but threatened masculinity is the reason that protecting their families in this way is so important to them (Carlson 2015; Stroud 2012).

All of this means that having a gun has become a potent symbol of masculine identity for at least some American men, and as we've shown, this means that men may decide to emphasize it in the face of threats to other aspects of their masculine identities. While a number of studies have looked at how individual men incorporate firearms into their gender identities, these have, for the most part, been ethnographic, dealing with relatively small populations. Such studies can tell us a lot about why the men in the study have guns, but they don't necessarily tell us a lot about broader trends, or about the world beyond the men the researchers are talking to. For instance, the fact that men in Texas consider gun ownership to be an important part of protecting their families doesn't mean that men in New York feel the same way, or even that men in Texas who weren't part of the study feel that way. Critically, much of the work that's been done on masculinity and gun ownership has been carried out in places with relatively lax restrictions on guns and a culture of gun ownership. It's entirely possible that guns function as a symbolic crutch for men's gender identities mostly in geographic areas in which guns are relatively common and their link to masculinity is well established. Unlike many of the other aspects of men's gender identities that we've discussed, it's possible that this one is practiced in some localities and not others.

The federal government does keep pretty good data on gun purchases in the United States, despite limitations on what can and cannot be reported to the public (for instance, Congress has prevented data on specific models of guns from being made public). The NICS system reports the number of firearm purchases in every state and the District of Columbia on a monthly basis, going back to 1998. While it's great that a unified data set on the subject is available, it has limitations. First off, it doesn't record the number of firearms being sold in a particular transaction: depending on state laws, it could be one or it could be 20; we just don't know. Second, it includes only purchases of firearms through licensed dealers, or other sellers that may be required by state and local laws to make use of the background check system. That means that, for the most part, purchases at gun shows and in other private transactions aren't included in the data. Essentially, the NICS data function as a basement estimate for the number of guns sold in a state, or nationwide, in a given month: we know the real figure is somewhat higher, but we don't know exactly how much higher. Third, some states use the NICS to carry out background checks on individuals applying for concealed weapon permits as well as for firearm purchases. This inflates the number of background checks in those states, but the number of new concealed carry applications is an order of magnitude smaller than the number of new gun purchases, and the states with the most concealed carry applications are also those that have the most firearm purchases. There's also no reason to think that the dynamics of concealed carry applications are markedly different from the dynamics of firearm purchases—indeed, past research has treated them as being conceptually similar in the way that they're tied to masculinity. All told, the NICS data have some limitations, but so long as we're interested in how the number of guns sold changes, rather than the exact number that are sold, the NICS data set works well enough, and far better than any other existing source.

Even a quick look at the graph in Figure 5.3 showing the number of background checks per month reveals some basic features of the series. For instance, sudden spikes in the number of background checks tend to correspond to heavy media coverage of mass shootings, such as the Sandy Hook Elementary School shooting in December of 2012. These spikes are contemporaneous with concerns about gun control legislation, which may explain the rise in background checks during the Obama administration, and the relative stabilization afterward (Cassino 2016). Also evident from the graph, and important to our analysis, is the seasonality of background checks. Background checks—and it seems, gun purchases—peak in December and at the start of hunting season. In our subsequent analyses, we control for these endogenous factors in order to better isolate the effects of the threat variables that we're interested in here.

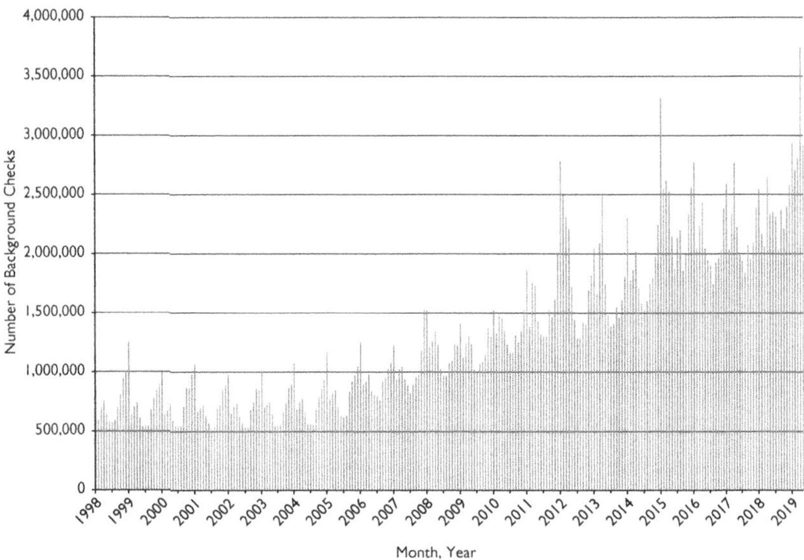

FIGURE 5.3: NICS Background Checks, by Month, 1998–2020.

In addition to the national NICS data, which are reported on a monthly basis, we also have annual state-level NICS data. We can use the national-level data to look at how changes in the degree of threat men are feeling change the number of background checks in subsequent months. But with the state-level data, we can look at contextual effects, to see how men in different states respond differently to those threat levels—something we simply can't do in the national data. At other places in this book, partisanship or ideology are used as mediating factors for similar analyses, but given the long time frame of these data, party doesn't work too well. For instance, Mississippi is one of the most conservative Republican states in the country today. But Mississippi had Democratic control in both houses of the legislature until 2010, and had unified Democratic control of the state from 2000 until 2003. By most measures, it was a more Democratic state than Massachusetts for most of the period studied, despite major differences in the ideological underpinnings of Massachusetts and Mississippi Democrats. Partisanship and political ideology mean different things in different states, and those meanings have shifted over the 20 years studied. So, instead, we follow the example of previous work on masculinity and gun ownership, and look at the prevalence of gun culture within a state. As noted before, gun ownership makes the most sense as a masculinity display in areas where it's a recognized form of masculinity, and in which laws and regulations make gun ownership relatively easy. To account for this, we make use of the number of firearms per capita in the state, a figure that's drawn from Bureau of Alcohol, Tobacco, Firearms and Explosives (ATF) data. These figures range from 3.8 guns per thousand residents in New York, to a high of 229.24 per thousand residents in Wyoming (the mean for states is 21.09 per thousand residents). These figures certainly represent some combination of the gun culture in a state, state politics, and existing state regulations, all of which are tightly linked, but what's important is that they tell us how likely a man is to see other people with guns, and how easily those guns can be accessed. In states where there are lots of guns and guns are easy to buy, threatened men are going to use guns as a compensatory masculinity more often.

As in many of our analyses, we're using unemployment as our marker for threat. Of course, there are lots of other reasons why men could feel threatened, but we lack individual-level data for these threats, whereas unemployment is regularly measured for an entire area. We are not, however, looking just at unemployment rates. As we discussed previously, loss of income or unemployment alone does not necessarily lead to threatened masculinity. The strongest threat seems to come from *relative* loss of status, and it is possible to isolate this in unemployment data. The idea is to look at the number of households in which married men are newly unemployed, while their wives are not. If the unemployment rates for married men and married women moved in tandem, that number would be zero: for every married man who loses his job there would also be a married woman who did. But if that number is positive, it means that there are married men who no longer have a job, while their wives do, and it's this group that we would expect to be under the greatest threat. Of course, this number will be driven, in part, by larger scale factors, like gendered unemployment rates and overall unemployment, so the model controls for those factors as well.

In the data, there are months in which 0.5 percent of men lose their jobs while their wives do not (the highest figure in the data set is actually 0.9 percent, but that's a bit of an outlier). The regression results tell us that, in that month, we would expect to see more than 100,000 extra background checks being carried out as a result. If married men had previously been doing better than their wives, the figure would be even higher. Again, we don't know exactly how many additional guns on the street this translates to: some of those background checks are for concealed carry permits, and a lot of them are for the sale of multiple firearms. What we do know is that this increased relative economic threat is leading more than a hundred thousand Americans, in one month, to do something to bolster their gender identity.

Using the state-level data, we can see how important the prevalence of guns in a state is to this behavior. In general, a 1 percentage point increase in the number of households in which men, but not their wives, have become unemployed, is expected to lead to a 0.2 percentage point increase in the number of background checks in that state that year. In large states, like California or Texas, that's about 20,000 extra background checks. But the more guns there are in a state, the stronger the effect: the effect is about 10 percent stronger in states with a moderate prevalence of guns, like New Hampshire or New Mexico, and as much as 70 percent stronger in states with a high prevalence of guns, like Wyoming.

In neither these analyses nor in the analyses of pornography use that follow, are we looking at individual-level behavior. Rather, we're looking at state- or national-level changes that we would expect to lead to gender threat, and state- or national-level measures that seem to represent ways in which men could respond to that threat, but none of this is on the individual level. This means that we cannot say, with any certainty, whether it is the men who have newly become unemployed who are buying the guns. All we can say is that in areas in which we expect more men to be under economic threat, more guns are being bought. So, it's possible that the state- or national-level threat conditions are leading to some kind of ambient threat in the area, which is leading to the behaviors, without working through the individuals facing the threat directly. This wouldn't change our interpretation of the results, as we're still looking at compensatory responses to threat, but because we're dealing with macro-level data, it's impossible to differentiate between such explanations. However, the individual-level theoretical background, as well as the individual-level results that we do have, strongly suggest an individual-level explanation, even if the data cannot fully establish it.

PORNOGRAPHY

Of the three topics covered in this chapter, pornography has the most obvious relationship to masculinity. When men feel their relative economic status is threatened, they become more likely to use pornography in general, and specifically more likely to use pornography that is dehumanizing or demeaning to women. When they can't assert dominance over women in the real world, it seems, men turn to types of pornography that allow them to do it symbolically.

While both men and women use pornography, heterosexual men constitute the overwhelming majority of consumers. In 2018, Pornhub, the most widely used pornography site in the United States, reported that its users were 72 percent male, with a mean age of 38 (see also Carroll et al. 2008, for more on pornography use among US men). Use of pornography may be common, especially now that high-speed internet access is available in US homes (Twohig, Crosby, and Cox 2009; Harper and Hodgins 2016), but individuals may be unwilling to admit to using pornography in surveys, especially high-quality surveys, which generally make use of live interviewers, who are disproportionately female. Moreover, even if we were to accept the survey-based estimates of pornography usage, those measures typically ask if a respondent has used, or uses, pornography, a measure that doesn't allow for within-person variation in usage. Put another way, people who use pornography may choose to do so at one time and not at another, and that variation isn't captured in a simple "use or not" question.

So, rather than rely on self-reported use of pornography, we make use of a direct measure: searches on Google for the most popular pornography website in the United States, Pornhub. As of 2019, Pornhub is the sixth most visited website on the internet in the United States, behind only Google, YouTube, Facebook, Amazon, and Yahoo!. Pornhub also puts out annual reports on usage of the site in various countries around the world, and on the demographics of users, allowing us to see what categories of pornography are most used by men and women in the United States (and around the world). Of course, we don't have access to the site's internal data, so we make use of the next best thing: Google searches, derived from Google Trends data. As Seth Stephens-Davidowitz (2017), who has used Google Trends data to study racism, has put it: people lie, but their Google searches don't.

Google Trends is based on a simple random sample of all Google searches within a specified geographic area, scaled to the overall number of searches coming from that area. Basically, more searches come from high-population areas like New York and fewer from low-population areas like Wyoming, so searches within Wyoming are scaled to overall use in that state, and searches from New York are scaled to the overall number of searches there. The geographically scaled searches are further scaled to the overall popularity of searches from that area, resulting in a 0 to 100 score that fluctuates based on the relative popularity of the search term within an area (after certain searches, like repeated searches from the same user for a given topic, are filtered out). This means that while Google Trends data can't be used to measure the number of people searching for a given term—it's not comparable across geographic areas—it can be used to measure the relative popularity of a search term within a certain area over time, which works perfectly for our purposes.

Of course, not everyone uses Google to find a website: individuals may bookmark a desired site, or simply type in a known web address. However, large proportions of Americans just don't seem to do this: the top Google searches for any year are terms like "weather" and "Facebook." It's not that the web address of Facebook or the Weather Channel has changed: it's just that Google is fast and reliable enough that it's easier to type "Facebook," or "Pornhub," or a recognizable misspelling thereof, and click the link, than it is to get to the site in some other way. Add to that the fact that users may not want to bookmark pornographic websites, and thus reveal to other users of a device that they're visiting these sites, and Google searches for a website become a reasonable proxy for use of that website.

Individuals also commonly make use of Google's search function to find content within a website. When you search for, say, "The New York Times," in addition to the link to the *Times'* homepage, you also get a search bar allowing you to search within the *New York Times*, saving you from having to use what might be an inferior search function within the *Times'* homepage. This existence of this Google search bar means that Google Trends can track not only the use of a particular website but also the relative popularity of topics within that site, allowing us to track the relative popularity of topics over time. The search data for Pornhub show significant variation among topics over the 10 years studied. For instance, controlling for searches for the website overall, searches for the "romantic" category are negatively correlated with searches for the "hardcore" category over most of the period studied (see Figure 5.4).

The Google Trends data are not without limitations. To preserve the anonymity of users, relatively rare search terms are not reported for small geographic areas. However, given the popularity of online pornography in the United States—Pornhub reports something on the order of 10,000

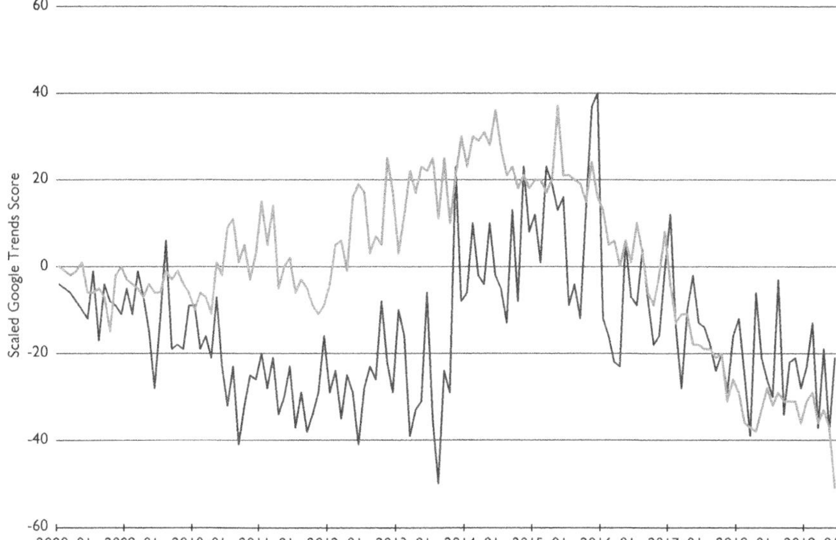

FIGURE 5.4: Google Trends Scores for "Romantic" and "Hardcore" Pornhub Categories, Controlling for Overall Searches.

to 20,000 unique US visitors to the site every minute—this isn't much of a problem for our analysis.

When we match up the Google Trends data with the same employment data we used previously, we can see the extent to which economic threats to married men are linked with increases in the use of pornography. A 1-point increase in households in which married men are unemployed, relative to the number of households in which women are employed (the same metric used in the study of gun purchases), leads to an increase of between 1.6 and 2.3 points in the Google Trends popularity of Pornhub in the subsequent month (the exact number depends on the specification of the model). As discussed previously, using this sort of lag in the data helps to establish causality: if an increase in married men's unemployment and an increase in pornography use were to appear at the same time, some other factor could be driving both. The fact that the unemployment rate changes happen *before* the changes in the rate of pornography use makes the alternate factor explanation less likely, and also eliminates the possibility of reverse causation (in this case, that increased searches for pornography led to a bunch of men getting fired).

How big is this effect? The scaling that goes into Google Trends data means it's impossible to translate point increases into numbers of website views or visitors. However, an increase of about 2 points across the United States, sustained for a month, is about the same increase in searches that would be expected from a successful national advertising campaign. Interestingly, it doesn't seem to be the case that more male unemployment, or even more unemployment among married men, always leads to more use of pornography. Increases in married men's unemployment, holding constant married women's relative unemployment, actually leads to a *decrease* in the Google Trends rating for Pornhub. It is only when married men's unemployment increases relative to married women's unemployment that searches for pornography increase.

To further confirm these effects, we make use of state-level data. If perceived economic threat is leading men to increase their use of pornography, it should be the case that states in which the economy is worse for married men will see larger increases in use of pornography, and states that have a better economic climate will not. While the Google Trends data allow for national monthly measurement of pornography usage, state-level economic data of the specificity we need are reported only annually. So, rather than the monthly Google Trends data for a state, we take the mean annual value for that state. The results of such an analysis largely confirm the monthly, national-level results: increases in the difference between married men's and married women's unemployment are correlated with an increase in the Google Trends ranking for Pornhub. The fact that we're using Google Trends data from different states, and thus scaled to different search volumes, within the same analysis means that the estimated effect of unemployment in the states isn't directly comparable to the national effect, but the numbers are pretty similar.

The state-level analysis indicates that the data aren't showing only that when married men's relative unemployment is going up an increase in searches for Pornhub follows. Because these unemployment rates are changing at different rates in different states, depending on the economic conditions in each state, the fact that the state-level analyses show the same relationship as the national ones increases our confidence in the story the data are telling.

But these analyses require us to make some assumptions about the users of Pornhub and the sorts of pornography they're viewing. We're assuming that it is men viewing the site, or at least, that the relative proportions of men and women using it don't fluctuate much over time (this assumption seems fairly safe: even across different countries, the

72 percent male to 28 percent female split currently found in the United States is pretty standard). We're also assuming that the users are heterosexual men, or again, that the proportion of heterosexual to homosexual users stays relatively stable. The biggest assumption, though, is about the types of pornography being viewed, but that's an assumption that we can directly test.

The theoretical work on masculinity and pornography leads us to believe that men are making use of pornography in order to symbolically establish dominance over women that they can't establish in real life. However, some types of pornography would seem to be much better suited to this purpose than others. Pornhub's top categories include some that would seem to be very much in line with a goal of dehumanizing or dominating women, such as "rough," and "hardcore." Others, like "romantic," do not align with that goal, and some, like "solo male," don't include women at all (categories like the latter seem to be aimed at homosexual men but are frequently viewed by women as well, according to Pornhub reports).

So, to the extent that men are making use of pornography in order to symbolically assert dominance over women, conditions of economic threat should lead them to some types of pornography but not others. We draw this distinction from previous lab studies looking at the effects of exposure to various types of pornography on men's attitudes. For instance, Malvina Skorska, Gordon Hodson, and Mark Hoffarth (2018) randomly assigned young men to watch two 10-minute clips of degrading pornography, erotic pornography, or for the control group, a news clip. These researchers defined erotic pornography as "non-degrading, nonviolent and consensual," in opposition to "non-violent, debasing and dehumanizing" degrading pornography. They found that young men randomly assigned to watch degrading pornography displayed more sexist and hostile attitudes toward women and had the highest levels of objectification of women. Exposure to erotica, compared to exposure to degrading pornography, created less objectification of the actors in the clips, but led to more willingness to engage in discrimination than was shown by participants in the control group. Using this definition of degrading pornography and looking at the categories most popular among US users of Pornhub, we identified three that seemed most likely to serve as symbolic expressions of dominance. All three generally include both men and women, graphic depictions of sexual acts, and discomfort or pain, caused by the male participant in the acts.

This result excluded categories like "romantic," which tend to feature nongraphic depictions of sex; solo videos, which include only one individual; and even popular categories featuring female same-sex relations, as they do not include men at all. Some categories featuring participants from minority ethnic and racial groups, often have characteristics similar to the three we selected, and even diminishment or dehumanization of female participants. When viewed by men from dominant racial and ethnic groups, such categories may serve a similar function to our three. However, they may also be used by members of the racial or ethnic group being depicted, for whom the appeal may be representational. As we have no way to distinguish between these uses, we removed these categories as well.

The same factors that led to increases in searches for Pornhub overall, and within the states, also led to increases in Google searches for the three categories that best fit our criteria. That is, increases in married men's unemployment rates, relative to those of married women, were correlated with an increase in searches for those categories within Pornhub. While we can't draw conclusions from the lack of an effect, it is telling that there were no such effects for categories, even very popular ones, that feature only female performers, or are less graphic. These categories must be popular for a reason, but they don't seem to be appealing to the same impulses that lead men to seek out pornography in which men graphically assert their dominance over women.

Interestingly, we did find similar effects in some specifications of the model for two other categories. One depicts mostly heterosexual sex with older women (identified as "moms," rather than "mature" women, which is another category entirely), and the other depicts African-American performers. It seems possible that the first of these is appealing on the basis of depicting women who are relatively powerful in society (as opposed to the very young women of most pornography or the much older women in some categories) being degraded in some way. The category depicting African-American women may be used by white men to symbolically assert dominance, as well, but these are, for us, post hoc explanations of an observed effect.

We should also acknowledge the potential problems with these results. Because the variables being measured are occurring in a geographic area (either the United States as a whole or an individual state), rather than on the individual level, we have no way of knowing whether there is a relationship on the individual level. It seems likely that the married men who have lost their jobs are the same ones who are consuming more pornography, and pornography of the particular categories we've been discussing, but we can't know that. Indeed, any study that did look at drivers of individual pornography consumption outside of the lab environment would likely face some serious ethical hurdles. But even if we decide that it is some threat in the overall environment, rather than a threat being faced by individuals, that leads to the increased use of pornography, the overall point remains the same: the use of certain types of pornography is a response to increased gender role threat.

Considered together, these three analyses allow us to put pornography use in much the same basket as the other compensatory behaviors we've discussed in this book. When men perceive greater threat to their gender identities, they make greater use of pornography, and especially those types of pornography that are demeaning or degrading to women. That may be objectionable for all sorts of reasons, but research on use of pornography also indicates that viewing pornography has long-term consequences for men. Research on the effects of pornography is often structured around the *hierarchical confluence model*, which holds that, in combination with existing personality factors, exposure to pornography can lead to increased sexually aggressive attitudes and behaviors. That is, reinforcing sexist and aggressive attitudes that men may already hold, may it more likely that they'll act on these attitudes.

These sorts of connections are backed up by studies showing a strong correlation between use of pornography in a region and rates of sexual assault and similar crimes. However, it's hard to establish causality in many of these studies because, generally, people select in to viewing pornography, making it possible that some outside factor is leading to both use of pornography and an increased likelihood of sex crimes (for instance, we would argue that gender threat among men could serve as such a factor).

In a 2015 experiment, Danish researchers Gert Hald and Neil Malamuth randomly assigned 201 adults (both men and women) under 30 years of age to see either 25 minutes of graphic pornography taken from films popular at the time or 25 minutes of nature documentaries. After watching the pornography, men—but not women—in the study scored higher on a scale measuring acceptance of violence against women, but this increase occurred only for those men with personality traits that already made them more likely to hold such views.

Use of pornography also seems to influence men's expectations about sex. Dan Miller, Kerry McBain, and Peter Raggatt (2018) used an experimental study to isolate the effects of men's pornography consumption on their perceptions of women's likelihood to engage in sexual practices depicted in pornography. Applying sexual script theory to sexual media socialization (see Gagnon and Simon 2005), Miller, McBain, and Raggatt argue that people's sexual assumptions are heavily influenced by media representations. They find that people who have been exposed to pornographic videos in the past six months are more likely to assume that women in similar settings and conditions are more likely to engage in porn-like sex. So, men who watch violent or degrading pornography may be more likely to attempt these sorts of sex acts with their partners in the future, and according to Miller, McBain, and Raggatt's work, may even be more likely to believe that women enjoy these acts. Such findings move the use of pornography out of the category of harmless diversion—if it ever was there—and into the category of potential societal concerns.

The three areas of religion, gun ownership, and pornography that we've looked at in this chapter all have a clear relationship to men's gender identities, and as a result, men use each of them as a way to reinforce threatened masculinity. It is, however, important to note that each of these areas is likely to appeal to different subgroups of men. The same factors that lead one man to embrace an identity as a born-again Christian are likely to make another man turn to pornography. While our use of macro-level data in most of these analyses means that we can't look at individual-level factors that might explain why some men turn to God and others to guns, the theory underlying our work does give us a good idea.

First off, we know that these compensatory acts must draw upon something that is important to the man in question. After all, the primary audience for all of these actions is the individual carrying them out: he's trying to prove to himself, as much as to anyone else, that his gender role is secure. So, a man who's never considered religion to be a part of his life is unlikely to respond to a gender role threat by embracing evangelical religion.

Second, the compensatory act should be something that is socially recognized—in the real world around him or in a virtual space—as being masculine. This is where the geographic effects of the gun models discussed come in: gun ownership is seemingly a balm to masculinity everywhere, but much more so in places where there are already more armed men walking around. As this would suggest, social recognition seems to increase the power of the compensatory act, even if some acts are hidden from view. So, using pornography may work as a compensatory act, but going to a strip club in the presence of other men would likely work even better. This implies that public compensatory acts should build on each other: the more men there are who carry a gun in public, the greater the payoff, in terms of gender role compensation, that men will receive from doing this. However, it remains possible that there is an upper limit to this effect, a point at which an act is so common that it loses any distinctiveness and is no longer a powerful signifier. For instance, in high schools in the 1990s, "virginity pledges" tended to influence the sexual behavior of teenagers (Bruckner and Bearman 2005), but only in schools in which a critical mass of teenagers took the pledge (more than about 5 percent), but not so many that having done so was common (more than about 20 percent). Similarly, we can imagine that carrying a gun might serve as a strong compensatory mechanism for men when there are enough men carrying guns for it to be recognized as a masculine act, but not so many that it's common, forcing men at that point to find some other way to express their masculinity.

Third, the compensatory act must be accessible. The research presented in this chapter seems to indicate that use of pornography is a common compensatory practice—but that's likely because of widespread high-speed internet connections. If men had to buy pornography from behind the counter at corner stores, or make trips to specialized shops, they would probably view it less frequently. Similarly, taking on a religious identity as a born-again Christian or evangelical is really only possible in areas with born-again or evangelical churches. And owning guns may be a powerful way to compensate for a damaged gender identity, but if guns become harder to get, fewer men will use them for that purpose.

This tells us a lot about the malleability of masculine identities. The same men, under different social circumstances, are likely to engage in very different behaviors to assert a masculine identity, and it doesn't seem to matter which ones they engage in. Almost any behavior that is linked to masculine identity and that meets the criteria we have discussed may be used as a compensatory mechanism. While men are likely to gravitate toward those behaviors already central to their idea of masculinity, they may well change what's important to their masculine identities to reflect what's accessible and socially recognized in their time and place. Put another way, the focus of men's efforts to assert their gender identities is endogenous to the methods by which they do it: if guns or religion are more widely recognized and easily accessible, men may well decide that those are now an important part of their masculine identity, while breadwinner status isn't as big a deal.

We should also note the important role of race in all these discussions. While we have been talking about "men" generally, much of the literature, especially that regarding firearms, indicates that some of the gender role compensation mechanisms discussed here are more prevalent among white men. While we would argue that the underlying model, in which men redefine their gender roles to compensate for threats, applies across racial groups, the individual behaviors are likely to vary widely between these groups. Nor is this point limited to racial groups: there is no universal definition of masculinity, so compensatory behaviors are likely to vary across any social groupings. Still, given the political and social power afforded to white men in particular, we think it valuable to start with them, and leave it to other, better situated researchers to see how the model applies to other groups.

CHAPTER 6

ALTERNATE MASCULINITIES

After reading the previous chapters, a reader could be forgiven for having a pessimistic view of men and their masculine gender identities. As we've seen, threats to masculinity seem to lurk around every corner, and even though there's still a long road to travel to reach equality between men and women in the United States, perceived threats are only becoming more common. Men see wives earning more than their husbands as a threat, even when those wives aren't theirs. Female bosses are a threat, as is even the possibility of a female US president. Even raising the possibility of nonbinary gender and sexual identities seems to constitute a threat.

And what do men do in response to these threats? They sexually harass women. They adopt more conservative political and social views, and turn against female candidates. They buy guns, and look at pornography that demeans women or join in born-again Christian movements. And as threats to men's dominance and gender identities mount, it seems as though these responses, many of which are far from socially desirable, will only get worse. The gendered ugliness we've seen in American society in recent years—with nominees for high office laughing off claims of sexual assault or rape, chants of "lock her up" that always seem to refer to politically powerful women, and mass shootings linked by the misogyny of the shooters—seems as though it may be just the start, as men find more ways to assert their gender identities in the face of a world that no longer gives them automatic dominance.

It seems bad. But in most of the analyses presented in the previous chapters, there are grounds to believe that it doesn't have to go that way. While modern masculinity is terribly fragile, it's also enormously adaptable, and some men are finding more socially desirable ways to reinforce threatened gender identity.

The overarching theory behind all the behaviors we've described is fairly simple. When men believe they are failing to meet an important aspect of their gender identity, they identify some other aspect of their gender identity that they *can* meet, and redefine their own conception of their own masculinity to stress that aspect. "I may not be *x*, but I'm still a man, and I can be *y*," they're saying, where *x* is someone who is a breadwinner, or is dominant in society, or has any status that presents threat, and *y* is someone who opposes abortion rights, or protects the family by having a gun, or plays the role of spiritual head of the household. Moreover, as we've shown, masculinity is highly adaptable, and *y* can be all sorts of things, including behaviors that may be more socially desirable than those we've explored thus far. As most clearly shown in our work on guns as a masculinity display, compensatory behaviors are enormously variable, and change depending on social context: what it means to be a man, and how men can demonstrate their gender identity, shifts over time and place, so there is plenty of room for new behaviors to take the place of the old compensatory strategies.

For instance, a long line of research shows that household labor, especially routinized tasks like cleaning and daily cooking, are seen as being feminine, and that men avoid these tasks as a way of asserting masculine gender identities (see, for example, Thébaud 2010; Goldberg 2013; Schneider 2012; and Thébaud, Kornrich, and Ruppanner 2019). Under conditions of threat to their identities, often coming in the form of a spouse who earns more than they do, men may wind up doing even less household labor than they otherwise would. "I might not be the breadwinner in the household anymore," we can imagine men saying, "but I'm sure as hell not going to do the dishes."

But while most household labor has largely continued along these lines, with men avoiding it as a way of asserting their masculinity, there does seem to be an exception: cooking. While men generally avoid routinized tasks like the daily preparation of evening meals, in recent years, there have been signs of a shift in how men view cooking. Why cooking, rather than vacuuming or doing laundry? Part of it has to do with a shift in how cooking is represented in US culture, and part of it has to do with openings already present in beliefs about masculinity.

The change in the representation of cooking in the United States can be traced back to one particular cultural import: the wildly over-the-top Japanese cooking competition show *Iron Chef*. Despite, or perhaps because of, its demonstrable foreign-ness and stylings reminiscent of pro wrestling, with entry music and multi-episode plot lines built around feuds between cooking schools, it was a surprise hit for the then-young Food Network (this phenomenon is discussed in Gallagher 2004). Before too long, this led the Food Network to shift almost entirely away from demonstration-based cooking shows, in which largely female hosts prepare food in sets designed to look like home kitchens, and in which the outcome is never really in doubt, to competition-based shows. In these competition-based cooking shows, which quickly colonized network and cable television alike, largely male competitors vie to demonstrate skill and risk-taking in a context where the outcome is always in doubt, and failures are excoriated by the judges. Even culinary-based travel shows began focusing on large portions of fatty foods (such as the long-running *Diners, Drive-Ins and Dives*) or on the consumption of foreign foods that might be intimidating to viewers (as in *Anthony Bourdain: No Reservations*). In short, "cooking" started to be presented as a masculine, rather than feminine, endeavor (Negra and Tasker 2019). Before too long, even Food Network shuffled its remaining demonstration-based shows off to a separate channel.

How can cooking start to be seen as masculine, while doing the dishes remains a feminine activity? The answer comes from cooking-related behaviors that were already embedded in masculinity narratives. Some forms of cooking, like cooking for special events, cooking with meat, and cooking on open fires, were already seen as masculine activities (Mechling 2005; Sobal 2005). As such, all it took to make regular cooking masculine was the addition of masculine ingredients, or of cooking techniques that showed technical mastery or risk-taking, and then making everyday meals could be masculine tasks. In past work (Besen-Cassino and Cassino 2014), we showed that over the course of the period between 2002 and 2010, coinciding with the shift in media portrayals, cooking went from something men rejected when they faced gender identity threat to a compensatory behavior. That is, by 2010, men who were facing gender threat at home started spending *more* time on cooking, the opposite of what they had been doing just a few years prior.

This shift is important because it shows exactly how malleable compensatory behaviors can be. If a behavior like cooking can easily go from something men avoid in order to express their gender identities to something men use as a compensatory behavior, it raises the possibility that other behaviors could evolve similarly, perhaps leading men to more socially desirable behaviors as ways of asserting their gender identity.

We told a similar story about the contextual nature of compensatory behaviors in our discussion of guns. While gun ownership exists as a compensatory mechanism throughout the country, it's a more common compensatory behavior in parts of the country where gun ownership is already more common. These compensatory mechanisms aren't inherent in masculinity: they're socially constructed, and so they can change along with society

This means that even though gender threat pushes the majority of men toward the sorts of behaviors embedded in hegemonic masculinity, it can also push some men in the opposite direction. So long as behaviors have some link to men's conceptions of what they're supposed to be doing, they can become a source of compensatory masculinities. Men who take the route of reinforcing gender identity through a wholesale rejection of what they consider to be the behaviors and attitudes associated with hegemonic masculinity seem to be a minority. It may be tempting to respond to a threat to gender identity by rejecting that identity entirely, redefining masculinity in a way that doesn't include the aspect that couldn't be met. But this sort of wholesale rejection seems to be less common than the approach in which men deprioritize the aspect of masculinity they're failing at, and instead stress a different aspect that they feel they're meeting. While this strategy means they're still embracing masculinity (and may not meet the hopes of some gender scholars), it also means that they may embrace more socially desirable behaviors and attitudes as compensatory behaviors.

There are signs of both these sorts of behaviors in the quantitative analyses discussed in previous chapters, but it can be difficult to sort out exactly what's causing the observed changes in behavior, especially with aggregated data. To see what these processes look like from the perspective of individual men, we have turned to qualitative data, drawing from our database of statements from men facing economic stress or unemployment and from their families, as well as statements from women about the behaviors and attitudes of men in their households. The statements were pulled from a systematic search of online narratives (including discussion boards and free-standing blogs) in which men speak about unemployment and their responses to it, carried out in the fall of 2018. All told, the search uncovered 400 distinct narratives, which were further divided into statements, some of which are excerpted here. (See the Methodology Notes for this chapter for further details on these narratives and how they were collected.)

In many of these statements, we can see how individual men square behaviors that they may not see as masculine with a masculine gender identity. The men represented in our qualitative data are mostly making use of the second strategy discussed previously, in which they embed the compensatory behaviors in other parts of their gender identity, which they selectively prioritize. For instance, Peter, who's been unemployed for some time, says:

> I try and do a lot of things around the house. I'm basically a "househusband." I shop, cook, clean, take care of our dog, etcetera, while she's at work. I also figure out things for us to do in the area for when she's not at work. For example, two weekends ago we went on a biplane ride over the city. We're going camping in the Everglades next week. . . . I try hard to make sure I'm not just slacking off all day while she's at work. She works three 12-hour days a week, which usually gives us plenty of time together to hang out or travel. After all, that is the reason we're doing this in the first place.

Peter is cleaning the house and taking care of things at home while his wife is earning the money. How does he square this with his masculinity? For him, the important thing is that he's not "slacking off," that he's working hard to be a good husband. By subsuming the feminine-coded acts of cleaning and dishes into what he's decided is the more important roles of hard worker and husband, he can do them without having his gender identity threatened. Also, note how he brings up the adventurous things he plans and carries out: camping trips, biplane rides. There's no clear reason to talk about these trips when he's ostensibly talking about being at home—except to say that being at home gives him the opportunity to do these things, allowing him to better fulfill an alternate masculine role.

Of course, such shifts don't always come easily to men. Doug, who's also been unemployed for some time, says:

> I'm not very good at hiding my depression, which I'm sure is bringing her down too. We fight at least several times a day now, which is taking a toll on us both. She feels like I don't help enough around the house or do enough to change our situation. Maybe this was true at the beginning but I've been doing more for a while now . . .

For Doug, not doing anything around the house is a major source of tension in his relationship. In essence, being a good husband is at odds with not doing housework. He's being forced to choose between violating his gender identity by doing the dishes, or violating his gender identity by not being a good husband. He would seemingly prefer to avoid the issue by not doing the housework and not getting called out for it, but when it's clear that this isn't a possibility, he starts doing the housework.

Doug's comments also reflect findings about differences in how men and women in the United States perceive the meaning of household chores. As University of California, Berkeley sociologists Arlie Hochschild and Anne Machung (1989) write, women perceive chores to be about much more than cleaning: they signal respect and care for the other person in the relationship. Doing chores, or not doing them, is a way of answering fundamental questions in a relationship, such as, "Do you love me?," and "Do you care about our life together?" From women's perspective, doing more chores signals commitment to a relationship. For men, it may signal a failure to live up to a masculine identity.

Not surprisingly, men who reported embracing household chores also reported that they were happier, and had happier marriages, for having done so. While some past research, based on data gathered in the 1990s, found that a more even sharing of the housework was associated with a lower frequency of sex (Kornrich, Brines, and Leupp 2013), re-evaluations with more recent data didn't find support for such a conclusion (Carlson et al. 2016). Indeed, sociologists have found that individuals who report doing more housework have more sex. Constance Gager and Scott Yabiku (2010), in their analysis of the National Survey of Families and Households, find that a 1 percent increase in men's weekly hours spent on housework is associated with a 0.06 percent increase in sexual frequency. That's not a lot, but the negative effects of not having a relatively egalitarian division of chores can be enormous. According to a 2016 Pew Research Center poll (Geiger 2016), sharing house chores is one of the top factors determining marital satisfaction. Fifty-six percent of married Americans say that the equal division of house chores is the most important factor in determining marital satisfaction (just behind "satisfying sex," at 61 percent).

Couples who don't have a clear system for dividing chores build resentment and report being much less happy in their marriages (Klein, Izquierdo, and Bradbury 2013). Using videotaped interviews and recordings of couples' interactions, researchers have found that a lack of clearly defined responsibilities leads to a power struggle over who will ultimately complete the task, turning the relationship into a zero-sum game, where one person wins by making the other lose. This helps to explain why unemployment leads to so much tension over household labor. When a man is no longer working, his wife is likely to expect that he'll do more chores around the house, altering their generally unspoken agreements about who should do what. When he doesn't, perhaps because of how he perceives the gendered nature of these tasks, tensions mount.

The narratives we collected paint a clear picture on this point. When men aren't able to square household labor with their gender identities, it creates conflict, as the men are trying to minimize the amount that they do, and thus minimize the gender threat. Their spouses, it seems, see them as being lazy, or can't understand why they won't carry out these seemingly basic tasks. This is often linked in men's written accounts to depression—used in the clinical or the colloquial sense—as the men feel the loss of their job as a loss of identity, and asking them to do work around the house threatens that identity even more. The fact that no one outside the house will know that they're vacuuming or doing the dishes doesn't matter: the primary audience for gender displays is the self. Self-defeating dynamics like this seem to be a big part of why loss of relative income is related to increased levels of infidelity and divorce in so many countries (González-Val and Marcén 2017).

But the narratives also give us examples, like Peter, of men who have found ways to redefine their gender identities to make room for household chores. These cases fall into two major groups. First, we have men like Peter who subsume household labor and other work that's coded as feminine into other behaviors that they consider to be appropriately masculine. For instance, attention to household labor makes for a happy spouse, hence it's part of being a good husband. It's also part of taking care of children, so they can justify it as being part of fatherhood. In essence, these men are acknowledging that household labor may be at odds with their gender identity, but are downplaying the importance of that conflict by making that labor part of a larger, more important aspect of their gender identity.

> I never, ever leave a mess in the kitchen. That shit backs up fast. I use the opportunity to model good behavior for my daughter, show her that I clean up after I'm finished with something. Even if it's 11 pm and I'm stoned and ready for bed, I put any stray dishes in the dishwasher.

The stay-at-home dad quoted here is among the many making similar connections: doing the dishes is necessary, not because it's part of cleaning the house but in order to set a good example for the children. Housework isn't itself important, but is rather subsumed into the larger idea of being a good father.

Unemployed men can also maintain a masculine gender identity while being stay-at-home dads by focusing on aspects of parenting that are compatible with traditional masculine identities, like mastery of technical skills, or ensuring a safe environment through home repairs and improvements.

> The other thing is I'm always looking for ways to improve our lives. Running a home is a skill so when possible I try and learn new things. I've learned new recipes, built and repaired things for our home, painted a mural for our son's room, and I learned gardening and grew some fruits and vegetables. Find something that is "you" and manifest it in a quality of life improvement somehow, don't be afraid to get expressive.

While we can't always see this in individual narratives, it seems likely that such views are the result of a re-ordering of the importance of various masculine ideals. Being a breadwinner may previously have been more important than being a good husband or a good father, but faced with the inability to be a breadwinner, these men seem to have decided that other parts of masculinity are more important. We saw a similar dynamic in the male leadership narratives of the Promise Keepers, and similar religious groups, telling men that breadwinning wasn't as important as other aspects of masculinity.

As an alternative to, or perhaps in addition to, subsuming housework into broader categories of masculine behavior, men may continue to treat household chores as feminine behaviors but compensate for them by doubling down in other areas. Many of the narratives about increasing the amount of household labor include references to other, masculine traits. Stay-at-home husbands brag about being strong enough to lift a couch or move a refrigerator in order to clean properly, or about how they made their own super-charged cleaning supplies (echoing the macho, high-fat, meat-based cooking discussed previously) so that they can clean better.

The issue of performing household labor may seem small in the face of the larger political and social issues that we've covered, but it's because it's such a small, familiar area that we can see so clearly how men can adapt their gender identities to encompass feminine-coded behaviors. If they can do so with such intimate behaviors—and certainly, not all men in the narratives we studied showed the interest or capacity necessary for this— then they may be able to do the same with other behaviors.

FATHERHOOD

Parenting certainly falls into the category of behaviors that were previously coded as feminine, as women's work, but men's embrace of parenthood as a compensatory masculinity act is one of the major themes in our content analysis. This may not seem like a development—parenthood is, after all, one of the pillars of middle-class American masculinity identified in the package deal (Townsend 2002); but what fatherhood actually entails for men has changed substantially over recent years.

Peter Townsend's qualitative work identifies four aspects of modern fatherhood: emotional closeness, protection, endowment, and provision. Emotional closeness requires that the father spends time with the children, protection that he ensures a safe environment for them, endowment that he gives them opportunities he may not have had, and provision that he earns enough money to support them. Protection, endowment, and provision are mutually reinforcing: by earning money, the father can do all three. This creates a conflict with emotional closeness, as spending more time at work and earning more money necessarily leave less time for fathers to achieve a close relationship with their children. As Townsend notes, men traditionally have resolved this bind with the help of stay-at-home wives, who took care of all of the day-to-day maintenance of the house and children, allowing the fathers to spend their limited time with the children in more emotionally fulfilling activities. By eschewing everyday contact, fathers were able to maximize "quality time" with the kids, thus letting these fathers do the fun, special things and achieve, at least subjectively, emotional closeness.

This model of fatherhood has been considered so desirable that men even get financial rewards for adhering to it. Sociologists Melissa Hodges of Villanova University and Michelle Budig of the University of Massachusetts find that fathers make more money than their non-father counterparts, all else being equal (Hodges and Budig 2010). They argue this "daddy bonus" is due to the important role of fatherhood in hegemonic masculinity. Fatherhood—or at least the traditional version of fatherhood—signals to employers that the candidates are loyal and dependable, leading to higher salaries and more responsibilities (see also Glauber 2008; and Killewald 2013). Ironically, these traits of loyalty and dependability mean spending lots of time at work, and even being available for work when you're not necessarily supposed to be working: traits at odds with being available to spend time with your children.

Today, however, men are reporting spending much more time with their children than in the past. In 2016, the average father in the United States reported spending 8 hours a week on childcare. A little more than an hour a day may not seem like a lot, but this is three times as much as the average father spent on childcare in 1965 (Livingston and Parker 2019). Despite this, fathers still spend about one-third less time with their children than mothers, on average, but this is one case where averages may be misleading. While the mean amount of time fathers spend with their children has gone up, so too has the number of children in households without a father (Livingston and Parker 2019). At the same time, the number of fathers who are primary caregivers, especially in the wake of the Great Recession, has increased. Unlike the men who are spending "quality time" with their children between work assignments in order to fulfill the demands of hegemonic package deal masculinity, these men are doing the feminine-coded everyday work of raising children. Looking at how these men balance the demands of full-time caregiving with masculine gender identities helps us see how masculinity can be adapted to meet the role of "stay-at-home dad."

The narratives we have collected seem to indicate that the easiest way for men to reconcile loss of income with masculine gender identities is through an insistence that, as stay-at-home dads, they are working, and are helping their family financially.

> You can do the math work and figure out your value to the family by adding up childcare, nannying, house maintenance costs. Factor in meals, shopping, reduced gas, reduced tax bracket, etc. Finally, you should consider the reduced anxiety your wife feels having you home and how much better it is for your kid to see their dad all day long. Those are costs, put a reasonable price on those and you'll find out you're not losing out on much money.

Stay-at-home dads may not be earning money, but by reducing childcare costs, they're saving the family a great deal of money. Of course, this argument that household labor is equal to, and should be valued as equal to, work outside of the home has been pushed by feminist activists for decades. In the view of our stay-at-home dads too, "women's work" should be considered real work, at least to the extent that men are doing it.

But because this shift in gender identity privileges other activities above being the breadwinner, the stay-at-home dad narratives can't just say that it's worth it because of the childcare savings. As one stay-at-home dad says: "What I do is more important than money, but at the same time, I'm actually helping a lot on the money side indirectly." Being a stay-at-home dad may mean that these men are saving their families a great deal of money, but, since being a father is more important than earning money, they have to reduce the importance of those savings.

The men in our narratives also square their status as stay-at-home dads with their gender identities by engaging in compensatory activities that, at first, lack any necessary relationship with parenting. While the narratives about being a stay-at-home dad have all sorts of advice, many of them also talk about the importance of exercise. Physical fitness is presented as necessary to keep up with kids, but also as an aspect of being a good parent: after all, a more fit dad is one who can play and engage more. Exercise—and especially weight-lifting—is presented as something men can do at home during nap times, as a way to clear their heads, regain focus, or work out stress and frustration. Fathers dealing with very young children are advised to use the children, and their carriers, as weights: "kid curls" are said to be lots of fun for the kids being lifted, while "working your arms and core to stay stable." Fathers are also advised to bring older kids into the exercise sessions, in order to set a good example.

One of our narratives featured a stay-at-home dad "looking for his masculinity," and finding it in compensatory activities, like exercise.

> I resisted Zumba class, instead taking time . . . to push some weights. Unbelievably, I wasn't any weaker, and I realized the physical strength earned at the gym finally had a practical application in my daily parenting duties. I didn't feel depressed like the studies suggested, and the only anxiety experienced was by my t-shirt sleeves.

There's obviously a lot going on here, but not only is the narrator claiming that his at-home weight training has made him physically stronger (as evidenced by the stretching shirt sleeves), but doing so made him a better dad, as being stronger has a "practical application" in parenting. Indeed, those practical applications mean that his physical strength is more impressive than that of men who lift weights or work out just to look good: his fitness is useful, while they're just being vain (a trait that is, after all, not compatible with traditional masculine identities).

This is far from an isolated case. University of Florida sociologist William Marsiglio (2016) finds that fathers have come to define themselves as caretakers of family health in recent years. Generally, men in the United States are less likely than women to take proactive measures to protect their own health. The physical toughness and stoicism that form part of hegemonic masculinity have traditionally led men to be less likely to seek medical help, control their diets, or make use of preventative medicine. However, he also finds that some fathers are central to promoting health and fitness behaviors in their children. While the subset of fathers he identifies is relatively small, and socioeconomically constrained (it may be easier for middle- and upper-class white men than it is for others to do this), their numbers seem to be growing. Healthy eating may not be part of traditional masculine gender identities, but physical strength and toughness is, and all this can be integrated into traditional gender identities through fatherhood. Again, we see an important gender role functioning as a kind of Trojan horse, giving men a cover under which to embrace socially desirable behaviors while maintaining hegemonic masculine gender identities.

NAVIGATING SOCIETY WITH NEW IDENTITIES

The men whose narratives we've been analyzing have found ways to reconcile behavior previously seen as incompatible with masculinity with their own gender identity. As far as they are concerned, their role as fathers or husbands makes them more masculine than men who are merely supporting their families financially. As one of the men whose narratives we read puts it: "I love being a stay at home dad. Nothing I have done in my life has been as meaningful or as fulfilling. I am willing to bet a lot of you can't say that about your career."

Indeed, the narratives often reflect a degree of surprise and dismay when others don't seem to see the men's roles this way. The stay-at-home dad narratives frequently discuss the social isolation these men experience, especially in encounters with stay-at-home moms and nannies who don't know how to fit such dads into their social networks.

> We get ready like any other parent. We have our diaper bag, bottles, diapers, snacks, toys and kids ready to go. Then we get to the play group and it happens. We are shunned. Instead of being welcomed like we had hoped, the moms look at us like predators, sure we are there to assault them or their kids. We aren't welcomed into play groups and many moms just keep their distance.

> As a stay at home dad the past 6 years, I've witnessed dads treated entirely different than moms. Commercially, everything caters to moms, with no intent to cater to dads who otherwise excel doing the same job. For the past 6 years, not one person other than family has bothered to help me with my children when it's evident an extra hand might occasionally be needed. I've had doors shut in my face while carrying my son, and holding my daughter's hand. If I was a woman, and or a mother, you bet people would run to help hold a door. Why can't the same be done for fathers?

The narratives do present a solution to such problems, in the form of stay-at-home-dad support groups, meeting either in person or online. In the online support groups, men vent about the sorts of difficulties they face as parents, and about the extent to which these challenges are unique to men. In the in-person groups, they organize outings and play dates for children, which they see as a necessary corrective to being excluded or marginalized in most groups, groups that they see as female-centric.

To some extent, narratives like the ones presented here bring us full circle. Many American men have come to believe that society is somehow tilted against them, that progress toward sexual equality means that men are being discriminated against, despite their overwhelming primacy in most political, economic, and social institutions. But here we have men who have successfully adapted their gender identities in order to meet the demands of society, who have taken on roles that were previously the domain of women, and they, too, believe that society is discriminating against them. In some cases, the men in these narratives are veering close to men's rights activism, discussing the need for protests and legal reforms to correct what they see as bias against men in the legal system, and especially, family court. Such views would not necessarily be problematic if they were not coupled, often, with open expressions of misogyny.

Men's willingness to adapt their masculine gender identities to embrace behaviors like housework and fatherhood makes more sense in light of the seeming alternatives to doing so. After all, what happens if unemployed men refuse to start spending more time with their children or to participate in household labor? While we don't have as many narratives from men in this situation, in those that we do have, men describe themselves as being depressed, and express their frustration with the failure of those around them to adapt to what they are experiencing as a disability. They also express dismay when they perceive that their spouses and others around them are now treating them differently. As far as they are concerned, they're the same men that they always were, and they're upset that they're being expected to take on new tasks and responsibilities.

The men in these situations may not talk about them much themselves, but we get a sense of others' reactions to their behavior from narratives provided by their spouses.

> I let him wallow for a bit and then I demanded that he do something. Anything: get a job, go back to school, pull the kids out of daycare and be a stay at home dad. He chose the stay at home dad route. He sucked at it. He never left the house. He barely engaged with the kids. They were miserable so I put them back on daycare

> and told him to go to therapy. . . . It is hard to respect a husband who won't even provide basic care to his children.

> I've been coming home worn out, and he'll have been playing video games all day, something he never really did except in fits and bursts, but now it seems to be some kind of coping mechanism, with most of the chores undone. . . . Not once in the two months have I seen him put together something on his own. I'm worried he's depressed.

The narratives from the wives describe a number of recurring elements: listlessness, disrupted sleep schedules, constant use of video games, unwillingness to do chores or take care of children. While these men may indeed be depressed, they also seem to be failing to cope with a sudden shift in how they see themselves, and how they perceive the world sees them. Being a breadwinner may well have been the cornerstone of their gender identities, and they're adrift without it. As many of these narratives indicate, this has profoundly negative consequences for marriages. The wives admit to a loss of respect for their husbands, as well as a loss of interest in sexual relations. This, of course, leads their husbands to a further downward spiral. While research has shown that men tend to overestimate the loss of esteem they'll suffer from unemployment (Michniewicz, Vandello, and Bosson 2014), these men may be accurately assessing the loss of esteem suffered from their *responses* to unemployment, if not from the unemployment itself.

The frequent references to increased video game use in the wives' narratives raises questions about the meaning of these games for the men. The video games may be serving to provide social connections with other men via online gaming options, or may be offering men the opportunity to act out masculine roles in a virtual world. They may even serve as a way for men to demonstrate mastery, even if that mastery involves the Mario brothers. More research on the gender-reinforcing role of video gaming would help to sort out these functions.

Long-term loss of employment and a new identity as a househusband or stay-at-home dad may be more likely than other kinds of gender identity threat to lead to a wholesale re-ordering of masculinity, because of the enormous consequences of a failure to adapt. Men who can't adapt lose the respect of their spouses, and often their relationships, because they aren't able to find a way to express their masculine gender identities in their new situation. Shorter-term unemployment, loss of relative income, or a perception of discrimination may cause a similar threat to men's gender identities, but the consequences of a failure to adapt to these situations may be less severe, or not as long-lasting as failures to adapt to long-term loss. Men in these latter situations may not need to engage in a re-ordering of the aspects of their gender identities, as the cost of doing so isn't justified by the lesser damage being done to their masculinities.

Taken together with quantitative evidence discussed in the previous chapters, these narratives help to show how men's gender identities can lead them to behaviors other than those prescribed by hegemonic masculinity. As we saw in Chapter 3, gender role threat leads most men to prefer more conservative policy views and male, rather than female, candidates. But it doesn't have that effect on *all* men. Men who have more liberal, or less sexist, preexisting beliefs become *less* likely to hold conservative policy beliefs, and *more* likely to prefer female candidates over male candidates. Relative to the size of the effects making men more conservative, these countervailing effects influence a relatively small proportion of men, and the effects on average move the opposite way. But these countervailing effects are real, and visible in the data.

Could the same factors that lead men to embrace housework and fatherhood also be leading them to embrace more progressive politics?

If we were to find that some men were doing so, it would mean that they were meeting the challenge laid out by University of Southern California sociologist Michael Messner in his 1993 treatise on "new men." In it, Messner argues that "shifts in style of masculinity do little, if anything, to address issues of power and inequality." That is, men may be more open about expressing feelings or doing more household labor or putting more time into fatherhood not because they're rejecting masculinity but in order to better assert it within a shifting cultural context. A true post-masculinity social and political movement among men, Messner writes, would confront men with the reality of the ways in which their standing in society relies on the subjugation of women, something that the men's movements of the 1990s observed by Messner were not doing. Men's movements like the Promise Keepers (described in Chapter 5) offered to help men get in touch with their feelings and bond with other men. However, Messner dismisses them as just a style of existing masculinities, papering over some of the problems that are causing difficulties for men rather than actually fixing any of them. As Messner argues, these movements served to reinforce the dominance of men, just in a way that's more palatable to these men's identities. As he also points out, men's groups that encourage men to get in touch with their feelings, and cry openly in the presence of other men, operate with the promise that this will help men be more successful in business and relationships. They're not crying because they've rejected hegemonic masculinity: they're crying in order to better attain hegemonic masculinity ideals.

Messner suggests that the true test of new, progressive political masculinities comes from the extent to which men's political views are effectively degendered, with men identifying with women as workers or as fellow citizens. As he notes, the vanguard of such a movement came from gay men, who were doing things like protesting in support of abortion clinics on the basis of identification with women as a group facing political oppression. In political terms, it seems that this would take the form of men stressing their role as allies, to women or other under-represented groups in their communities. We didn't find a lot of narratives that talk about political activism, but we did encounter a spate of men talking about their role in the feminist movement in the wake of the well-attended Women's Marches in 2017. Simon, a stay-at-home dad, stresses this role as an ally, as someone subordinate in feminist movements.

> It was only since becoming a father of a daughter that I took the time to see the world from a woman's perspective, and was appalled at what I saw. Things I didn't understand were issues became clear. I certainly class myself as a feminist, but as a man I also understand the need for me to listen to women rather than enter into and try and dominate any conversations.

While Simon does mention his daughter, and the impact that she had on his worldview, he's not saying that he needs to participate in political activism in his role as a father. He's not saying that being a good father, or a good husband, requires that he work with feminist groups to try to make a better world for women close to him. Rather, he's saying that being a father led him to recognize that things were bad for women, and led him to try to do something about it.

Twenty-five years after Messner's insights, and with some evidence that at least some men are embracing the more progressive political positions that Messner hoped for, has masculinity met Messner's challenge?

Our conclusions are mixed. In the quantitative data, we find evidence that some men are responding to threats to their masculine identities in exactly the way that Messner would have hoped: holding more positive views of minority groups, and women's rights, like Simon, in the narrative excerpted here. But it's not clear *why* they're doing this. Some are, perhaps, rejecting hegemonic masculinity, and working to create a level playing field for men and women. Others are re-ordering their masculine gender identities to stress roles that they can attain, like the men who talk about the importance of doing dishes in order to be good fathers. So, stay-at-home dads may volunteer to help the PTA or run for the school board as part of their identity as a father, or participate in a Women's March in support of their identity as a good husband. Still others may be rejecting traditional masculinity entirely, and forging a new gender identity based on a whole new set of identities.

The narratives from and about unemployed men seem to suggest that re-ordering masculine roles is the most common strategy employed by men under conditions of gender identity threat. Rather than question the basis of their gender identity, they find the aspects of accepted masculine gender identities that they can attain, and focus on them. This re-ordering allows them to take on behaviors and attitudes that are otherwise inconsistent with hegemonic masculinity, without really questioning that underlying identity. Indeed, as we've seen, they may even believe they're doing better at fulfilling their gender identity than men who are hewing to traditionally masculine behaviors.

What does this look like in the outside world? In the wake of revelations involving the assault, harassment, or other mistreatment of women, recent years have seen the rise of a genre of statements from otherwise conservative politicians in which they frame a response in terms of their relationship with one or more women. For instance, in 2016, Senate Majority Leader Mitch McConnell responded to the tape of then-presidential nominee Donald Trump bragging about sexually assaulting women by saying, "As the father of three daughters, I strongly believe that Trump needs to apologize directly to women and girls everywhere." Former Florida Governor Jeb Bush responded to the same scandal by saying, "As the grandfather of two precious girls, I find that no apology can excuse away Donald Trump's reprehensible comments degrading women." When Harvey Weinstein was forced out of his movie studio by allegations of assault and worse, Matt Damon, who had worked with him closely, and was accused of having killed a story that shed light on Weinstein's behavior earlier, spoke "as the father of four daughters," when he said that Weinstein's behavior was upsetting.

The typical response to such statements is harsh. After all, sexual assault and other reprehensible behavior from men should be appalling to everyone, regardless of their relationship to women. These statements make it seem as though the man in question is saying that *he* is not really offended or upset by the behavior, but that his role as a father or grandfather or husband means that he has to take it seriously.

Our analyses of statements from stay-at-home dads in this chapter give us a different way to evaluate such statements. Just as stay-at-home dads talk about how it's important to cook for their kids as part of their role in keeping everyone healthy, or how cleaning the house is important to being a good husband, these men talking about their daughters or granddaughters or wives are making statements about the relative ordering of masculine roles in a given situation. The stay-at-home dads are saying, sure, cooking may be a feminine task, but being a good husband is an important masculine task, and if it requires that I cook, that takes precedence. Similarly, men making these statements about harassment and assault are saying that even if they might understand or overlook such conduct in their social role as men, their competing social identities as fathers or husbands require that they condemn it.

Now, these sorts of statements are clearly not meeting Messner's challenge to men to be allies to women outside of a gendered identity. It's also troubling that anyone should feel a need to qualify why mistreatment of women should be a concern: why not just condemn the behavior and leave daughters and granddaughters and wives out of it? But, as we've seen, while there is some evidence of a backlash against hegemonic masculine identities, most men today are still unwilling to entirely leave behind the negative aspects of masculine gender identity. These responses, though, are a way for these men to condemn some of the negative aspects of hegemonic masculinity while still maintaining conventional gender identities themselves. Would it be desirable for them to simply condemn sexual harassment or assault, or worse? Of course. But however they get there, they are getting to the same place, just in a way that tends to reinforce their existing gender identities. It's a half step forward for these men, but a step forward nonetheless. While it represents imperfect progress, it is progress, and perhaps the most likely way for such progress to be achieved.

CHAPTER 7

THE FUTURE OF MEN

In *The End of Men*, Hannah Rosin (2012) argues that male dominance of society is coming to an end. In her argument, the increased anxiety of men is justified, and the erosion of men's social and economic privilege is just an early sign of greater changes to come. Men's historical advantages, in her telling, arose from their being better suited to the sort of work that was driving the economy: factory work, manual labor, farming, tasks that required upper body strength. The traits needed then are less important for the jobs that now dominate the economy, so men's dominance is fading. But such an argument doesn't help us to account for entrenched male dominance at the highest echelons of the corporate and political worlds, or the continued wage gap between men and women in the same jobs.

Rosin explains such situations by arguing that the advantages still held by men are vestigial, and are on their way out. And by many measures, women do seem to be catching up with men, though there's still a long way to go. But even though our society is nowhere near equality, which would mean men and women being on a level playing field, movements toward equity lead men to experience gender threat, and that threat leads them to push back. The compensatory behaviors that we've described throughout this book are part of that response, as men, not necessarily as part of an organized social or political movement but as individuals, search for new ways to express their gender identities.

Despite the range of compensatory behaviors we've described, we believe that we have only scratched the surface of an understanding of how gender threat drives men's behavior. Everywhere we've looked, we've found evidence for men responding to threat by doubling down on some behavior designed to bolster their gender identities, and there's every reason to believe that there are far more examples yet to be found.

But as interesting and important as the various examples we've uncovered have been, it's their cumulative impact that matters most. Together, they tell us a lot about masculinity, and perhaps, about how men are adapting to a rapidly changing society.

Research and theorizing about men's gender identities goes back more than a century, and in that time, scholars have generally reached a consensus about masculinity. Men, like women, have a gender identity. That identity is more relevant at some times than at others, and if that identity is called into question, men react, taking action to assert their masculinity. These assertions often involve doubling down on some aspect of their gender identity that they feel that they can prove, and the primary audience for these assertions consists of men—both the individual and the men around him.

Over the course of this book, we've tried to flesh out this understanding, by bringing different techniques into the study of masculinity and gender threat. We've made use of large data sets so as to detect smaller effects that might not be visible on an individual basis. We've used survey experiments and time series studies so as to make better claims on cause and effect. Based on the entirety of our results, we believe that we can reach some general conclusions about men's gender identities, how they respond to gender threat, and how those responses are changing.

A number of our studies have made it clear that the actions men take to bolster their gender identities have no necessary relationship with the threat itself. For the most part, work on masculinity threat has looked at individual environments, and how men perceive threat, and bolster their identities, within those environments. For instance, when men perceive a female boss as being a threat to their gender identity, they may become more likely to harass her or other women in the workplace. This isn't a reasonable response, by any means, but we can see the relationship between the threat and the response: men experience gender threat in the workplace, so they find a way to assert their masculinity in the workplace.

We can see similar effects in lab studies. In a 2005 study, men completed a task that was described as "hairstyling" to one group and as "rope reinforcing" to another; men in the "hairstyling" group became more likely to assert their heterosexuality (Bosson, Prewitt-Freilino, and Taylor 2005). The participants may well have associated, or thought others associated, hairstyling with homosexual men, and responded to such a threat by verbally asserting their sexuality. There seems to be a relationship here between the source of the threat and the response to it.

In many of our studies, however, that nexus simply isn't present. In areas where men experience greater levels of economic threat, gun sales increase. Men who have lost income relative to their spouses become more likely to oppose abortion rights. These responses have no necessary relationship with the source of the threat, save that both the threat and the response draw on the individual's view of his own gender identity. Economic threat leads men to believe that their masculinity is in jeopardy, and politics and guns are potent ways for them to express their masculinity.

In some ways, we could see these relationships as troubling—why should opposition to abortion increase in response to economic threats?—but it also raises some interesting possibilities. We've also discussed the socially desirable ways that some men have found to express their masculinity in the face of gender threat: if an overt relationship between the source of the threat and the compensatory behavior men use is not necessary, then men may be able to use these more desirable behaviors to compensate. If a man responds to gender threat by harassing women at work or buying a gun, it may be a problem. If he responds by spending more time with his children or going to the gym, society may well be better off.

Our studies have also shown that while masculinity is enormously adaptable, it is also socially constrained. Men's ideas of what sorts of behaviors and attitudes can function as compensatory behaviors seems to be bounded, at least in part, by what can be recognized as masculine in the men's existing social context. Owing to the nature of most of the past research on gender threat in men, this wasn't evident: qualitative studies are normally limited in their geographic scope, as is any study that brings participants into the lab. In our studies, this is shown most clearly in the conditional effects of economic threat on gun purchases. In areas where guns are more common, economic threats to men produce a much larger increase in gun purchases than these same threats do in areas where guns are less common. While there may be some male behaviors that are common across a culture, like the rejection of some kinds of household labor, there's also the opportunity for enormous variation. Like the use of guns as a compensatory behavior, religion may work best as compensation in areas where certain denominations are more common, and cooking may serve as a compensatory behavior mostly in areas where certain food cultures have taken root. This opens up exciting new areas for researchers, who can look at how men respond to gender threat differently in different social contexts. In some of those contexts, men are likely pursuing more socially desirable compensatory behaviors than in others, and understanding this variation may help us in understanding the interaction between the individual's understanding of gender and society's understanding.

Our findings also hint that assertions of masculinity don't have to be public to be effective. Most of the work on men's responses to gender threat centers on the idea that men engage in compensatory behaviors in order to demonstrate their masculinity to those around them. Think of the groups of men ogling female co-workers in Beth Quinn's research: by participating in this form of harassment, they're demonstrating their masculinity and heterosexuality to their male co-workers. The public nature of the demonstration is the point (Quinn 2002). Similarly, the firefighters quoted by Jonathan Deutsch (2006) used sexualized descriptions of foods to demonstrate to other firefighters that even though they doing the cooking, it didn't make them any less masculine. A refusal to do housework or an increased propensity to affiliate with a traditionalist or evangelical sect may reinforce masculine identity only in the home, but there's still an audience. However, not all the behaviors that we've come across in our studies have an outside audience. For instance, when men are facing greater economic threat, we see an uptick in the use of certain genres of pornography that may be seen as more degrading to women. It doesn't seem likely that men are widely discussing their use of pornography with other men, so the audience seems to be the individual. When men embrace fatherhood, they may be demonstrating a masculine identity to their spouses or others around them: but when they stress certain aspects of fatherhood, like managing their children's exercise or eating habits, their work is largely invisible to outsiders. Gun ownership may be a quasi-public demonstration of gender identity, but carrying a concealed weapon, a related behavior that's been linked to expressions of masculinity, is by definition hidden from public view. Such demonstrations of masculinity seem to be less about showing off to others and more about men showing off to themselves. We have no reason to believe that these audience-less compensatory behaviors are any less effective in reducing gender threat than more public demonstrations. This means that understanding gender threat, and how men react to it, requires that we understand both how men present themselves to others and how they view their own actions: perceptions that are likely shaped by their beliefs about others, whether those beliefs are accurate or not.

In much of the past research on gender threat in men, assertions of masculinity and homophobia were tightly linked. Demonstrations of masculinity and demonstrations of heterosexuality were often taken to be the same thing, as in the "rope reinforcing" experiment and in much of the research on sexual harassment in the workplace. But while there is some evidence that men are treating heterosexuality and masculinity as being interchangeable, our studies have also found some evidence that this link may be fading. Outward expressions of heterosexuality among men could arise either from assertions of sexual interest in women or from the denigration of homosexual men, but both of these behaviors have become less acceptable in most US cultures in recent years. For example, when we examined the effect of loss of relative income on men's political attitudes, we found that it led them to be more opposed to abortion rights for women and more opposed to government assistance to African-Americans, but not more opposed to rights for homosexuals. Similarly, when we asked men to rate their gender identities, we found little connection between expressions of masculinity and expressions of heterosexuality among men.

Why? The reason for this is likely the enormous shift over the past decade in how homosexuals are perceived in US society. Denigrating homosexuals is simply less socially acceptable, on the whole, than it was previously, and so while some men may still hold negative beliefs about homosexual men, they may be less willing to express them openly. As we've seen, men have plenty of ways to express their masculine gender identities in the face of threat, but denigration of homosexuals may no longer be one of them for many men. This not to say that perceived accusations of homosexuality aren't threatening—recall that asking men about their sexuality on a survey affected their later answers about gun ownership and religious affiliation—but that the expression of negative attitudes about homosexuals may be much less central than it was in the past.

While men's views of what is and what is not masculine may be changing, our studies have found that past understandings of masculinity still exert some control over these newer conceptions. Masculinity may be enormously adaptable, but newer expressions of masculinity seem to be tied to traditional expressions. For instance, we've found that cooking has shifted in recent years from an activity that men would avoid in the wake of gender threat to one that they embrace as an expression of masculinity. This transition was aided by a shift in the way that cooking was presented in the media, but it also would not have been possible if cooking had not already been an acceptably masculine behavior under some circumstances. Because cooking meat-based meals and cooking on special occasions was already seen as masculine, men could come to see everyday cooking as being masculine as well, as men could make every meal something special or incorporate more meat products. Fathers making a point of being in charge of health and nutrition for their families is a new development; but it's premised on the traditional masculine virtue of physical strength and the masculine role of being a protector. Simply put, what seem like new masculinities aren't cut from whole cloth, but are accepted because they can be linked to traditionally accepted models of masculine behavior. The old models of masculinity may not be working anymore for many men, but they're not being thrown out: rather, they're being adapted. Certain behaviors that make sense for men get stressed and become an important part of the way in which these men express their gender identity. Attitudes and behaviors that can't be adapted in this way are downplayed or discarded. While new ideas about men's gender identities and how they are constituted and about new compensatory behaviors may be increasingly important to masculinity, we can't ignore the old ideas, which are still shaping the new.

Our studies have also shown the extent to which men's social identities have begun to blend together. Traditional notions of social identities hold that these identities—gender, race, sexuality, partisanship, and so on—exist largely in isolation from one another. Under some circumstances, they may reinforce each other; at other times, they may put cross-pressures on an individual, forcing him or her to privilege one identity over another. However, our work on the mingling of men's gender identities and their political identities raises the possibility that these identities may become so linked in social discourse, or in the minds of individual men, that they operate essentially as different expressions of the same identity. We found that for many men, expressions of masculinity and the eschewing of femininity were closely linked with the expression of partisanship. For those individuals, apparently, being masculine is synonymous with being a Republican, while femininity is synonymous with being a Democrat.

Though she makes use of a very different way of measuring gender identity—self-reported adherence to a long list of gendered traits built up over years of research in psychology—Fordham political scientist Monika McDermott (2016) finds that while women are more likely to support Democrats in US elections, controlling for sex, masculinity makes people more likely to support Republicans. So, US women's increasing levels of masculinity—remember that in our data women placed themselves as much more masculine than men placed themselves as feminine—could mean that the Republican Party is advantaged in future elections. Women may erode some of men's social and political dominance by adopting more masculine traits, but in McDermott's analysis, these same traits are likely to lead them to be more likely to vote like men, as well as increasing their levels of political participation. The accepted wisdom is that the increasing social and political power of women is good for the Democratic Party—but the strong link between gender, rather than sex, and political preferences may mean that it's not that simple.

Our studies have also shown the extent to which assertions of one's masculine identity can be used as a cover to allow men to pursue behaviors that aren't in line with traditional masculinity. This was demonstrated most clearly in the narratives given by men to explain their seemingly nonconformist behaviors: a stay-at-home dad referred to cleaning the house as part of being a good dad and cooking as part of being a good husband, and politicians frequently use formulations like "as the father of two daughters" to introduce views at odds with traditional masculinity. Because masculinity is multidimensional, and men can shift the importance of various elements within it, many behaviors that would otherwise not be considered masculine can be held up as examples of masculinity. There are, of course, limits on this sort of behavior. All the examples we found are tied to at least one of the core elements of American masculinity as discussed by Peter Townsend in *The Package Deal*: marriage, employment, home ownership, and fatherhood. Just as past understandings of masculinity still exert pressure on how masculinities can be adapted to new circumstances, it seems that a plausible relationship to traditional notions of masculine behavior is still needed for these adaptations to work. Moreover, even if men use what amounts to gender identity jujitsu to turn behaviors and attitudes at odds with traditional masculinity into something plausibly masculine, scholars like Messner would argue that they're not fixing anything, as they really need to stop viewing society through a gendered lens altogether.

While we've shown that men make use of various compensatory activities to assert their gender identities in the face of threat in all sorts of contexts, all these responses can be understood within a fairly simple theoretical framework.

First, masculinity is relatively fragile. Although the extent of their belief varies, men do believe that others will call their gender identity into question if they fail to live up the standards of hegemonic masculinity; this despite the fact that few men actually do meet these standards. These expectations are partly social, but they're also deeply internalized, with men consistently overestimating how much others will see them as not being sufficiently masculine.

Second, when men's gender identity is threatened, they make use of compensatory activities to assert their gender identity in response. These compensatory activities may or may not have a clear connection with the source of the threat. In either case, they essentially allow men to redefine their masculinity, reducing the relative importance of the threatened activity, and increasing the importance of the compensatory activity in their personal definition of masculinity. For instance, a man who uses symbolic religious authority to compensate for an inability to earn as much money as he feels he needs to earn has decided that religious authority is more important than being a breadwinner.

Third, these responses are meant to demonstrate men's masculinity to a dual audience, consisting of both others and the men themselves. Many of the best documented compensatory activities seem to be displays to other men, like many instances of sexual harassment in the workplace, or the carrying of a firearm. However, other activities are private, like the use pornography, or arguably, the carrying of a concealed weapon. Because the expectation for masculine behavior is largely internal, getting the approval of others for a compensatory activity may reaffirm it in a man's eyes, but this approval may not always be necessary. The important thing is that the man knows he's asserting his gender identity, whether others know it or not.

Fourth, the nature of these compensatory activities depends on the existing attitudes and identities of the men using them. Men with different predispositions—like the Republican men and the Democratic men in our political examples—are likely to respond to gender threat in different ways, leading to attitude polarization rather than a uniform shift in one direction or another. This also means that context is enormously important: what might work as a display of masculinity in one area, or among one social group, might not work in another. While some compensatory activities are widely understood as such, there are likely many more that are particular to social, racial, religious, or ethnic groups.

Fifth, activities can be newly defined as masculine provided they are linked with activities or ideals already seen as masculine. While people in general have an idea of "traditional" masculinity, that idea is constantly shifting in response to the social environment. As men spend more time with their children, child-rearing becomes a masculine activity; during the COVID-19 crisis, some men asserted their masculinity by refusing to wear a face mask. Refusal to wear a face mask might well be seen by those doing it as a reasonable compensatory activity in the context of an outbreak—men showing that they are unafraid, and trusting in their self-reliance and physical strength—even though this activity would have been unrecognizable as compensatory only weeks or months before. Any activity that can be plausibly linked with existing ideals or activities of masculinity—as in the example of cooking—can be redefined in such a way that it can be used as an expression of a masculine gender identity.

While we have established a theoretical underpinning for understanding compensatory activities, there is much that remains to be studied. We've seen a reference to a seemingly strong connection between threatened men and video games, but we simply don't know if that link is driven by threat or by boredom. Do certain kinds of games function as compensatory activities, while others do not? What do we make of the social aspects of many modern video games, with their voice chats and organized leagues? Do potentially undesirable, and even violent, behaviors learned in these games become more likely to leak out into the non-virtual world when used for these compensatory functions?

Similar questions arise from the use of social media. Journalistic accounts have sounded the alarm about spiraling extremism resulting from seemingly innocuous technologies like YouTube's recommendation engine. Are men using social media as a compensatory behavior? Are they using a virtual world to act out in ways that would be unacceptable in the real world? What are the consequences of these behaviors, and what can regulators and social media companies themselves do to monitor, and perhaps ameliorate, these behaviors? Researchers have shown how the use of pornography can have impacts on men's behaviors in the nonvirtual world—does the same principle apply to socially and politically extreme views encountered online?

The important influence of social norms on how men express their masculinity has been seen in behaviors like gun ownership. But more works needs to be done to identify smaller scale masculine cultures. There may be a cultural idea of "guys in Brooklyn," but are these men really different from other men? If so, in what ways? Can these differences be exploited to push men toward more socially desirable ways of expressing their gender identities? What other local cultures of masculinity exist, and what can we learn about masculinity in general by understanding them? It seems possible that qualitative work—interviews and ethnographies and focus groups—may be the best way to understand these local cultures, and really understanding how local cultures have changed may help us understand how masculinity is shifting in our broader society.

There's also the possibility that masculinity can help us understand deviant behaviors, like criminality and drug use, among adults and minors. Disentangling causation in areas like these may be difficult, but if men are using criminal behaviors to assert their masculinity, understanding men's gender identities may ultimately prevent crime and reduce recidivism. Workplace sexual harassment is linked with threats to men's gender identities; it's plausible, then, that sexual assault and rape and perhaps violence more generally are as well.

It also seems that the #MeToo movement has changed the relationship between sexual harassment and reporting. Has this changed the fundamental relationship between masculinity threat and harassment? The data simply aren't in yet, but research that looks at this could prove enormously important going forward.

Finally, it's vital that researchers, especially in political science, but in sociology, criminology, and psychology as well, do a better job of measuring gender. While we all pay lip service to the idea that sex and gender are different things, too many studies just don't measure gender, instead conflating it entirely with sex. On the theoretical level, researchers understand that gender isn't the same thing as sex, that it's multidimensional and that it has effects independent from those of sex, but that understanding is not often enough put into action. The biggest barrier to understanding how men's gender identities are shaping their lives is that we're not measuring those gender identities. That needs to change: our methods need to catch up with our theory.

Recent years have seen an explosion of interest in studying men's gender identities in the United States. Early indications are that men in other parts of the world behave similarly in response to gender identity threat. Since masculinity is a cultural construct, we can expect that both the factors that lead men to believe that their gender identity is being called into question and the actions that they may take to assert their gender identity in the face of that threat will vary between countries, but that doesn't mean there won't be any similarities. For instance, we took one of the studies discussed in Chapter 3, in which we induced gender identity threat in respondents through question about relative household earnings, and used a translated version with a sample of respondents in Mexico. As in the United States, breadwinner status is a staple of Mexican masculinity, so the question did lead to shifts in the stated political preferences of the Mexican respondents. However, rather than pushing them toward more conservative political attitudes and parties, it increased the likelihood that Mexican men would express support for the current President of Mexico, Andrés Manuel López Obrador (often referred to as AMLO). On the one hand, this seems like a change from the responses of men in the United States, who become more likely to assert a Republican, and pro-Trump, political identity when threatened. On the other hand, while AMLO is considered to be on the left side of the political spectrum, he's also a populist who has made use of many of the same claims and even some of the same policies as Trump. And even where their policy goals may be different, the political and rhetorical style of these two leaders is very similar. This suggests that gender identity threat isn't leading men generally toward conservative policy positions, but rather toward leaders who themselves assert masculine identities.

Similarly, while we have not carried out studies in Canada, Amanda Bittner and Elizabeth Goodyear-Grant (whose work was discussed in

Chapter 4) have carried out extensive studies of gender identity in the Canadian electorate. Many of their findings echo what we've found in studies of the United States: men with strongly masculine gender identities have relatively distinct political views, and these are exaggerated among men who say that their gender identity is important to them. Aside from their research, there has been pioneering work in Northern Europe, much of which has been able to take advantage of data sources (like prescription drug use) that aren't easily available in the United States, and which shows men's responses to gender identity threat there.

Continuing this line of research internationally as well as in the United States, and working on comparative models of gender identity threat and compensation, will certainly aid in our understanding of how men construct and defend their gender identities. Perhaps more importantly, though, it may also provide us with a path forward. If men everywhere have to deal with the same anxieties of gender, but men in some societies have found ways to channel those anxieties into socially desirable actions, there's no reason why we can't learn from them. The end goal of research on masculinity must be to help build a society in which men's gender identity is put toward positive productive ends, and looking at other societies could be a big step in that direction.

While men's expressions of masculinity have been shown to be tremendously adaptable, we have also seen how threat can lead to all manner of personal, political, and social behaviors, many of which may be socially undesirable. Masculinity can, and has, changed, but many, and perhaps most, men in the United States still cling to traditionalist ideas about their gender identities. Even as some men change the way in which they express their gender identities, others may perceive greater and greater levels of threat, as male privilege continues to erode. Making matters worse, the belief that gender relations are a zero-sum game—meaning that many men will assess any gains made by women as a loss for themselves—hasn't gone away, and may well be on the rise. Michael Messner and Nancy Solomon (2007), for example, point to debates over Title IX, the regulation that requires colleges and universities to provide an equal number of scholarships for male and female athletes. The rule mandates equality by sex—but that hasn't stopped men from arguing that they're disadvantaged by it, and that equality in scholarships is unfair to men, denying them opportunities they feel they should have. In their view, men have a greater innate desire to play sports, so treating men and women equally denies some kind of natural inequality. This view is hardly limited to sports. It also appears in the perception that if men are better workers, it makes sense to pay them more, and pay equity is tantamount to discrimination. If men are better artists and writers, then female representation in those fields means that qualified men are being shut out. If men are better leaders, it makes sense that they should be in charge of governments and corporations, and that movements for sex equity in legislatures and boardrooms are discriminatory. Such perceptions feed into a belief that men are under siege, leading to the sorts of compensatory behaviors we've described.

This may seem like a negative prognosis, but remember: masculinity is changing, it is adaptable, and it does respond to social pressure. Men express their gender identities in ways that are acceptable to their social groupings, and so, as society changes, expressions of masculinity will change as well. Yes, sexual harassment in the workplace seems to be driven by some men's need to assert their gender identity, but sexual harassment is down substantially. As society as a whole and individual workplaces have become less accepting of it, men have apparently found other ways to express their gender identities. Masculinity is changing, and it will adapt, with men finding ways to express their gender identities in ways that we can't yet predict.

APPENDIX

METHODOLOGY NOTES

CHAPTER 2: MAD MEN AT WORK

To measure the effect of national-level unemployment on changes in rates of reported sexual harassment, we used the FOIA data made available by BuzzFeed (aggregated to a monthly basis) and monthly unemployment data provided by the Bureau of Labor Statistics. It is relatively straightforward to look for changes in the unemployment rates and then to see whether the rates of reported sexual harassment increase or decrease in apparent response, and we include this basic model along with the analyses presented later.

The unemployment rate used here is the most widely reported (U6) rate, and fortunately, for providing variance in our data, it ranges widely during the period studied, mostly due to the Great Recession of 2008 and 2009. Over that period, it averaged 7.4%, with a median value of 7.45 (standard deviation 1.73, 10th percentile at 5.1%, 90th percentile at 9.5%). In an analysis looking at threat to men's economic status, it might be tempting to look at gendered unemployment rates: that is, men's versus women's unemployment. In this case, however, doing so would introduce some confounds into the relationship: if men become differentially unemployed, they may be more threatened and more prone to engage in sexual harassment, but having more women in the workforce relative to men may also lead to more opportunities for sexual harassment. Thus, we have chosen to use the overall unemployment rate. While the gendered unemployment rates do not move exactly in tandem, they are closely linked ($r = 0.88$), making the overall unemployment rate a good proxy for the unemployment felt by either sex.

However, this basic model ignores some critical aspects of the time series we are dealing with. For instance, the harassment rates have some endogenous aspects: standard time series diagnostics reveal autoregressive components at lags of 1 and 2 months, which should, ideally, be controlled for before we introduce exogenous factors.

Additionally, the amount of reported sexual harassment has trended down significantly since first being tracked, and we can account for this overall trend as well. This factor can be included as a simple year count variable (implying a linear decreasing trend).

We use ARIMA-based regression in order to control simultaneously for endogenous and exogenous factors in the model, and we use multiple specifications, moving from simpler to more complex, to allay concerns that specific modeling decisions are driving results. In an era in which social science researchers are increasingly concerned about *p*-hacking (Ulrich and Miller 2015; Head et al. 2015; Simonsohn, Simmons, and Nelson 2015), the presentation of multiple specifications can be useful. To the extent that all the specifications give a consistent picture of the effects of the independent variable of interest on the dependent variable we are modeling, we can be confident that the results are not being driven by the exact specifications of the model.

We present the results of four models of sexual harassment. Model 1 and Model 2 use the overall level of sexual harassment in a month as the dependent variable, as a function of the unemployment rate in the previous month. In Model 1, we exclude significant endogenous factors; in Model 2, these factors are included. Models 3 and 4 use the month-to-month change in the level of reported sexual harassment as the dependent variable (rather than the total amount of reported harassment), as a function of the change in the unemployment rate in the previous month. Because we are working with the differenced form of the dependent variable here, controlling for endogenous factors is rather more important than it is with the non-differenced form used in the first two models; including some parts of an ARIMA model (the differencing) without including others (the autoregressive factors) would be inconsistent, so the autoregressive factors are included in both Models 3 and 4. However, to help ensure robust results, we include the linear time indicator as an independent control variable in both Models 3 and 4. The results are presented in Table 1.

The first two models (one with endogenous autoregressive features of the series, one without), give a consistent estimate of the relationship between the overall unemployment rate and the overall level of harassment reported to the EEOC. While many robustness checks (such as jackknife estimation) are not appropriate for time series models, estimation of standard errors using the Huber-White sandwich estimator shows very similar results in Models 1, 2, and 4, though not in Model 3. Estimation using OIG or OIM techniques leads to the same conclusions as the standard models already presented.

However, because other factors could be leading both of these figures to be higher at the same time, a better test comes from looking at the relationship between changes in the unemployment rate and changes in the number of reported sexual harassment cases. In the two models using the differenced form of the variables, a 1-point increase in the unemployment rate in a month was expected to lead to a 5- or 6-point (depending on whether or not the linear time effect is included) increase in the number of reported sexual harassment cases in the following month. Put another way, an increase of one standard deviation in the unemployment rate (1.7 points) is expected to lead to an increase of about one-third of a standard deviation in reported sexual harassment in the following month. Note that ARIMA models, like the ones used here, do not estimate overall goodness of fit statistics for the model. Pseudo-R^2 estimates for these models range from 0.08 to 0.36, depending on the specifications used.

CHAPTER 3: MEN AND POLITICS

The first study consists of a survey experiment (n = 859) carried out via a live caller RDD survey (cell and landline), from March 11 to 16, 2016, among registered voters in New Jersey, by the Fairleigh Dickinson University (FDU) Poll.

Half of the respondents in the sample (n = 343) were primed to think about the increasing number of households in which women earn more than their husbands, before they were asked about their presidential election preferences. The item, asked only of respondents who reported being married, or in a marriage-like relationship, said: "There are an increasing number of American households in which women earn more

	Model 1		Model 2		Model 3		Model 4	
Dependent variable	*Harassment*		*Harassment*		*Change in Harassment*		*Change in Harassment*	
***R*-squared**	**0.15**		**0.28**		**0.34**		**0.35**	
	Coef	**Std Error**	**Coef**	**Std Error**	**Coef**	**Std Error**	**Coef**	**Std Error**
Unemployment (lagged)	**5.237**	**1.160**	**5.432**	**2.029**			**9.572**	**3.268**
Change in lagged unemployment					**3.517**	**1.782**	**0.726**	**0.315**
Linear time effect					0.125	0.087	**0.759**	**0.289**
Constant	131.752	8.650	130.93	15.287	–252.147	175.862	–1532.936	584.067
AR (1)			0.246	0.116	–1.011	0.014	–1.014	0.139
AR (2)			0.208	0.133	–0.999	0.002	–0.999	0.002
Sigma	21.020	1.610	18.315	1.234	17.548	1.343	16.774	1.374

TABLE 1: Number of EEOC Harassment Reports: ARIMA Models.
SOURCE: BuzzFeed data.

money than their husbands. How about your household? Would you say that your spouse earns more than you, less than you, about the same, or is your spouse unemployed?" Afterward, these respondents were given a distracter task, in which they were asked to name the first word that came to mind to describe the likely major party nominees for president. Then, they were asked two items about their preference in the (then upcoming) presidential election. In one, they were asked to choose between Hillary Clinton and Donald Trump; in the other, they were asked to choose between Bernie Sanders and Donald Trump. The order of these two election choice items was randomly determined, with half of respondents receiving one item first and the other half receiving the other item first.

The respondents in the other half of the sample ($n = 351$) were given the two items about their candidate preferences before the question about relative earnings was asked of the ones who had reported being married or in a marriage-like relationship (with the distracter task in-between).

Weighting was used to match the sample to known age, race, and gender characteristics of registered voters in the state. The weighted sample was 50% male, 14% African-American, 13% Hispanic, and 4% Asian-American; 23% were under 35 and 34% over 60. Fifty percent of the weighted sample were Democrats; 30 percent were Republicans. While this is a substantial edge for Democrats in party identification, it is in line with the characteristics of voters in what is a generally Democratic state.

Note that the actual results of the item asking whether respondents earned more or less than their spouses are not used in our analysis. There are two reasons for this. First, a remarkably low number of men in the sample (less than 5%) said that they earned less than their wives, with another 27% saying that they earned about the same. This meant that there weren't enough men admitting that they earn less than their wives for a reasonable analysis. Second, given that the known proportion of men earning less than their wives is much, much, greater than the figures reported in the survey, it also seemed likely that many of the respondents were simply lying, which would render any analysis unreliable (essentially, it would be differentiating between responses, rather than actual respondent characteristics).

Clinton was preferred 52 to 36 overall in the match-up with Trump, and Sanders was preferred 51 to 36 overall, a finding in line with other surveys taken in the state at around the same time.

In addition to the significant results reported in Chapter 3, there was also a statistically significant difference between the primed and unprimed groups in the proportion of respondents who refused to answer the match-up questions. In the unprimed condition, 8% refused; in the primed condition, 0% did so.

The second survey experiment was embedded in a national live caller RDD survey (cell and landline), with a total sample of 1,009 respondents, carried out by the Fairleigh Dickinson University Poll between April 13 and 18, 2016.

Respondents were asked a series of four questions about gender roles (including items like what proportion of members of Congress are women, and whether women are treated more or less harshly than men by the media). Half of the respondents received these four items immediately before the series of items asking about their preferences in head-to-head match-ups between presidential candidates, and half afterward. The experimental condition had a main effect, but the effects discussed in Chapter 3 are the conditional effects, in which the experimental condition had a different effect for individuals who feel that the media treat women less harshly than men and for those who feel that they treat women more harshly than men.

Logistic regression was used to predict the likelihood of voting for the Democratic nominee in a match-up with Trump.

Analysis with the same independent variables shows no significant effect of the experimental condition, either in the main effect or in the interaction, on support for Sanders in a match-up with Trump (see Table 2).

The Data For Progress survey, carried out in June 2019, surveyed 2,953 likely Democratic primary voters, selected through a screening process. While samples drawn from online panels are non-probability samples, the panel is large enough that, when proper weights are used, it can approximate a probability sample of the general public. Before weighting, the sample was 57% female, 47% college educated, 10% Hispanic, and 17 % African-American.

The sexism scale used was constructed from four items, each measured on a 5-point scale, ranging from Strongly Agree to Strongly Disagree:

Most women interpret innocent remarks or acts as being sexist.
Women are too easily offended.
Most women fail to appreciate fully all that men do for them.
Women seek to gain power by getting control over men.

DV: Support for Clinton	Coef	Std Error	z	P>z
Exp. condition	−1.802819	0.546517	−3.3	0.001
Harshness judgment	−1.108717	0.196433	−5.64	0
Condition × Harshness judgment	0.7365221	0.270891	2.72	0.007
White?	−0.8206161	0.280094	−2.93	0.003
Education	−0.00363	0.054744	−0.07	0.947
Age	−0.0110677	0.005221	−2.12	0.034
Black?	−0.1133068	0.371113	−0.31	0.76
Unemployed?	0.6293893	0.355097	1.77	0.076
Party ID	0.9006261	0.064606	13.94	0
Sex	0.0321332	0.206006	0.16	0.876
Constant	0.7930109	0.670998	1.18	0.237

TABLE 2: Support for Clinton: Logistic Regression.

Responses to the items were equally weighted, and scaled to a range of 0 to 1, with 1 indicating strong agreement with all of the items, and 0 indicating strong disagreement with all of the items. Overall, 25% of the sample scored a 0 on the scale (the modal outcome), which had a mean of 0.27, a median of 0.19, and a standard deviation of 0.254. We considered respondents to have a low score on the scale if they scored a 0 on the scale, a moderate score if they were above 0 but below the mean value, and a high score if they were above the mean value.

While the experimental manipulation of having respondents pick between two female candidates was not intended, the randomization of candidates means that it works just as well as if it had been. The conjoint experiment characteristics were randomly assigned to the match-ups, such that individual sets of characteristics could be repeated between (but not within) match-ups, so the same respondent could see the same set of characteristics multiple times, though never the same match-up; 1,324 of the 2,953 respondents (44.8%) were asked to choose between two female candidates at least once, and thanks to the vagaries of random assignment, one respondent was asked to choose between 5 different sets of female candidates (he had generally favorable views of them, giving himself an average motivation of 8.4 to vote for them in a general election match-up).

After saying which of the candidates they would prefer in the match-up, respondents were asked which of the candidates could beat Trump in a general election match-up, with "neither" and "both" included as response options.

Then, the respondents were asked about their motivation to vote for the candidates in a general election match-up with Trump, on a 0 to 10 scale: "On a scale of zero to ten, where zero represents not at all motivated and ten represents very motivated, how motivated would you be to vote for [Candidate]?"

Overall, respondents rated their motivation to vote for the candidates at a 7.08, with a median value of 7.3 (standard deviation 1.98). Male respondents were slightly, though not significantly lower, with a mean score of 7.01 (median 7.3, standard deviation of 2.14); female respondents gave themselves a mean motivation of 7.13 (median 7.2, standard deviation 1.85).

All differences reported in the text are significant at $p < .05$, two-tailed (except those that specifically note they are not significant). Simple *t*-tests, rather than regressions, were used for the comparisons reported in the text.

The survey also randomly assigned respondents to see the attributes of the candidates (race/ethnicity, age, sex, environmental policy views, "insider" status, and healthcare policy views) in one of four different orders. In two of those orders, the sex of the candidate was the first or second attribute presented; in the other two, it was third, the last of the demographics to be presented—1,493 respondents got the sex of the candidate in one of the first two slots; 1,460 (49.4%) got that information in the third slot.

The analysis of within-participant change in political views comes from the 2006–2008–2010 GSS panel. Because the panel includes the period in which men disproportionately lost jobs, relative to women, a significant number of the men had significant income losses, relative to their wives. That allows us to examine how the stated political views of men change in response to loss of relative income on a within-subjects basis. In essence, the analysis uses loss of relative income as an intervention, and allows us to see how the political views of men who lose income relative to their spouses change between periods of the panel. The results show that loss of income significantly alters the views of men, but only on issues tied to dominance of other groups (abortion, for instance). On these issues, the loss of income makes Republican men more conservative and Democratic men more liberal.

The results are based on 3-way interactions in the data between changes in relative income, the party identification of the individual at the start of the period, and the constant dollar household income at the end of the end of the period, with the dependent variable being the change in the variable of interest. Because the same individual could be counted multiple times in the data set (for the 2006–2008 period and the 2008–2010 period), clustering was used to correct the standard errors for the actual number of respondents. There were a total of 1,708 men in the data, though the actual *n* for each analysis is a bit smaller, owing to missing data in one or more of the waves.

The respondent's views on abortion were measured using an 8-point scale (running from 0 to 7), based on responses to various scenarios in which a woman might seek an abortion (for instance, if a woman does not want more children, or if a woman cannot afford more children). A respondent who said that abortion should be available under any circumstance, answering "yes" to all seven items, would be scored a 7. One who thought that abortion should never be allowed would score a 0. The mean score on this scale was 4, with a standard deviation of 2.5. The mean movement between waves of the study was only 0.003 points, making a case for its relative stability as a measure. Eight percent of respondents dropped by 3 points or more on this measure between waves, 16% dropped by 1 or 2 points, 19% increased by 1 or 2 points, and 4% increased by more than 2 points on the scale.

Views on government aid to African-Americans were measured through an item that asked respondents to agree or disagree with the statement, "Irish, Italians, Jewish and many other minorities overcame prejudice and worked their way up. Blacks should do the same without special favors." Overall, 41% of respondents "agreed strongly" with this statement, and 5% "disagreed strongly." As with abortion, there was very little change in the mean response of the sample, but 26 % of respondents moved 1 or more points toward disagreement on the 5-point scale, and 10% moved 1 or more points toward agreement.

On marriage equality, 15% of respondents overall "strongly agreed" that homosexuals should have the right to marry one another, with 32% saying that they "strongly disagreed" with that statement. Unlike with the other measures, though, there was a change on the 5-point agree-disagree scale between waves, with the mean score moving 0.1 points toward agreement between waves (reflecting the general societal shift toward that position in the period studied). Twenty-one percent of respondents moved 1 or more points toward disagreement between waves, with 27% moving toward agreement.

The dependent variable in each analysis is the change in the respondent's answers on the same policy question between the two periods. In each case, the analysis controls for the year in which the data were collected, the age of the respondent, whether the respondent was married at the end of the period, whether the respondent had divorced during the time between interviews (about 2% of the sample), and the three main variables of interest: absolute income (measured in constant dollars at the end of the wave: mean of $51,500, standard deviation $42,600), change in relative spousal income, and party identification (at the beginning of the wave being analyzed: measured on a 0–6 scale, mean 2.75). Interactions between these three variables were also included, along with all constituent (2-way) interactions needed for meaningful interpretation of the three-way interaction. (See Table 3.)

For the purposes of the figures presented in Chapter 3, "lower" relative income means a drop of 39 points relative to the spouse: for instance, a drop from earning 80% of the combined income to 41% of the combined income. This is the 80th percentile of income loss for those men who lost income. Put another way, it's the 10th percentile of change in relative income. "Increased" relative income is a gain of 39 points, which is at the 90th percentile.

CHAPTER 4: SEXUAL ORIENTATION AND GENDER IDENTITY

For the national FDU Poll discussed, carried out in late May 2020, the overall sample size is 1,003. Respondent's sex was asked within the survey, rather than being guessed at by the interviewer, with an option for nonbinary respondents; 51% of the respondents were women. Respondents were asked about their gender identity on a 6-point unidimensional scale, running from "completely masculine" to "completely feminine." Forty-eight percent of men and 46% of women identified as "completely" masculine or feminine, with most of the remaining identifying as "mostly" in the gender category in line with their sex. The exact wording of the instructions was as follows:

> The traits that we see as being masculine or feminine are largely determined by society, and have changed dramatically over time.

	Marriage Equality			*Govt Aid to African-Americans*			*Abortion Views*		
	N: 402	Pseudo R^2: 0.01		*N*: 416	Pseudo R^2: 0.01		*N*: 398	Pseudo R^2: 0.02	
	Coef	Std Error	z	Coef	Std Error	z	Coef	Std Error	z
Year	0.316	0.190	1.66	–0.089	0.189	–0.47	–0.249	0.192	–1.29
Age	0.010	0.005	1.74	0.003	0.005	0.58	–0.011	0.006	–1.93
Divorced?	–0.288	0.057	–0.50	0.265	0.482	0.55	1.717	0.529	3.25
Married?	0.071	0.203	0.35	0.003	0.212	0.01	–0.109	0.207	–0.53
Constant relative income	0.000	0.000	1.26	0.000	0.000	–1.39	0.000	0.000	–0.20
Constant absolute income	0.000	0.000	–1.53	0.000	0.000	0.11	0.000	0.000	–0.89
Change in relative income	0.956	0.058	1.64	–1.709	0.734	–2.33	–1.424	0.583	–2.44
Constant absolute income × Change in relative income	0.000	0.000	–1.97	0.000	0.000	2.44	0.000	0.000	2.01
Party ID	–0.124	0.009	–1.41	0.074	0.087	0.85	–0.115	0.088	–1.31
Constant absolute income × Party ID	0.000	0.000	0.78	0.000	0.000	–0.03	0.292	0.000	1.32
Change in relative income × Party ID	–0.191	0.117	–1.63	0.428	0.253	1.69	0.428	0.117	2.50
Constant absolute income × Change in relative income x Party ID	0.000	0.000	1.98	0.000	0.000	–2.08	0.000	0.000	–2.17

TABLE 3: Effect of Income Change on Political Views.

> As a result, everyone has some combination of masculine and feminine traits, which may or may not correspond with whether they're male or female. How do you see yourself? Would you say that you see yourself as Completely Masculine, Mostly Masculine, Slightly Masculine, Slightly Feminine, Mostly Feminine, or Completely Feminine?

The data presented in Chapter 4 made use of a 6-point scale, not because of any inadequacy in Bittner and Goodyear-Grant's 101-point scale, but because these simpler scales can capture most of the variance found in the more complex scales. Similarly, there is no strong theoretical reason to prefer an even-numbered scale with no neutral center point to an odd-numbered scale with a neutral center point, though even-numbered scales may be desirable in samples with larger than normal proportions of respondents from SOGI minority groups.

These results match up well with the work of Bittner and Goodyear-Grant (2017a, 2017b). They found almost the same proportions of both men (39%) and women (36%) identifying with the extreme gender category congruent with their sex, and found about the same proportions of respondents in the gender categories conventionally associated with the other sex (8% in their sample, 11% here, mostly women in both). Given the differences in survey mode (online versus live caller) and population (Canada versus the United States), these similarities are striking, and support the idea that the 6-point scale is generally capturing the same construct as the larger scale.

The results also align well with McDermott's multidimensional BSRI data, which are drawn from a US online sample (McDermott 2016). In these findings, individuals with high levels of femininity are more likely to identify as Democrats, while individuals with high levels of masculinity are more likely to identify as Republicans, with a stronger relationship between femininity and being a Democrat (24 points) than between masculinity and being a Republican (18 points). In comparison, our data find that individuals at the highest level of masculinity are 18 points less likely to identify as Democrats, and 18 points more likely to identify as Republicans. While the unidimensional nature of our measure means that we cannot differentiate between McDermott's "undifferentiated" and "androgynous" categories, the partisan distribution of individuals in these categories is very similar to the distribution of individuals in our middle

	Masculinity Scale		Femininity Scale		Combined Scale		
Percentile	**Men**	**Women**	**Men**	**Women**	**Men**	**Women**	**Overall**
10th	69.0	3.0	0.0	62.0	70.5	61.0	66.0
25th	74.0	9.0	5.5	73.0	74.2	73.0	73.5
50th	87.0	19.0	14.0	82.0	85.3	81.5	85.0
75th	93.5	29.0	22.0	92.0	95.2	91.5	91.5
90th	100.0	40.0	30.0	97.0	100.0	96.5	100.0
Mean	83.8	19.9	15.5	81.6	84.2	80.9	82.6
Std dev	13.3	15.1	12.3	14.0	12.4	14.3	13.4

TABLE 4: Self-Reported Femininity and Masculinity, by Reported Sex.

("slightly") categories, with the biggest group of these individuals in the Democratic category, the second largest group in the Independent category, and relatively few Republicans. (See Table 4.)

Respondents were also asked how important being a man or a woman is to their overall identity, on a 4-point scale, running from "extremely important" to "not important at all." Forty-three percent of men and 55% of women said that it was "extremely important," with most of the remainder in the next category, "somewhat important." This measure was inspired by the work of Bittner and Goodyear-Grant (2017a) showing the differential impact of gender identity by the reported importance of that identity to the individual.

For our 2018 experimental analysis, the exact instructions for the masculinity and femininity scales were slightly different from those given for the telephone sample above, and are presented in full in Figure 4.4.

The online survey also included a unidimensional sexuality preference scale, on which respondents were asked to rate their attraction to members of their own sex versus attraction to members of the other sex. Responses to this scale had very limited variance, and thus were not used in the analyses. At the suggestion of a conference participant who saw this research presented, we have moved to a two-scale format for such items in later surveys.

The analyses reported here were carried out on a non-probability MTurk sample of 125 Americans (residence confirmed by provider). The respondents were paid $1 for their time, and spent an average of 5.8 minutes on the survey, for an hourly equivalent rate of $10.34. The sample was 51% male, 46% married (17% never married), 16% under the age of 30, 66% aged 30 to 44, and 15% aged 45 to 59. Sixteen percent of the sample had only a high school diploma, 34% had a bachelor's degree, and 14% had a postgraduate degree. Ninety-three percent of the sample was white, and 4% were African-American. Six percent identified as Latinx. In sum, the respondents were less likely to be elderly than the overall US population, slightly more educated than would be expected, given the age of the respondents, and rather whiter than would be expected in a random sample of the US population. These characteristics are in line with past analyses of MTurk samples.

While samples such as this have been criticized for being non-representative, it has been established that they are much more representative and diverse than traditional convenience samples (Casler, Bickel, and Hackett 2013), and more attentive to instructions and unexpected tasks (Hauser and Schwarz 2016), which was useful for this study. Recommended steps (higher pay, less filtering of eligibility of respondents) were taken to try to increase the representativeness of the sample (Silberman et al. 2018). In sum, while we don't believe that the sample represents anything approaching a simple random sample of the US population, it is superior to sampling techniques that have been widely accepted for the study of psychological processes for decades, and is appropriate for the research questions at hand.

To analyze the effects of the experimental condition, an ordered logit analysis was used, with each participant's self-placement on the 7-point party identification scale (using a standard two-step item, scored on a 1- to 7-point scale, with 1 representing Strong Democrat, 4 representing Independent, not leaning toward one party or the other, and 7 representing Strong Republican) as the dependent variable (mean score of 4.8, median of 4, 9% Strong Republican, 20% lean/not-so-strong Republican, 15% independent, 20% lean/not-so-strong Democrat, 29% Strong Democrat). Predictors in the analysis were the experimental condition, the participant's score on the combined masculinity-femininity scale, the participant's reported sex (1 = Male; 2 = Female), and all the interactions between these three.

The results of the regression show that the experimental condition has a significant effect on expressed party identification, but only in concert with other factors. Percentage effects reported in the chapter text are the

Predictor	Coef	Std Error	z
Condition	–4.90	3.15	–1.56
Combined scale	–0.05	0.02	–2.50
Sex	–4.79	2.50	–1.92
Condition × Scale	0.07	0.04	1.76
Condition × Sex	7.61	4.30	1.81
Scale × Sex	0.06	0.03	2.12
Condition × Scale × Sex	–0.10	0.05	–1.99

TABLE 5: Expressed Party Identification: Ordered Logit Regression.

result of using the Stata "margins" command to convert these coefficients to marginal expected effects. (See Table 5.)

Note that while the main effect of the experimental condition is not significant, this indicates only that the condition does not have a significant main effect once we control for the conditional effects included in the interactions. The main effect of interest, and the one driving the results presented in the chapter text, is the three-way interaction effect presented in the last row of Table 5.

There is no significant difference in the overall mean values between the experimental conditions. Overall, participants in the control condition gave themselves a mean score of 82.6 on the combined scale (which includes the scores on both the masculinity and femininity scales, relative to the sex of the respondent), while those in the experimental condition gave themselves an 82.5. Even when the sex of the respondent is accounted for, there is little difference between the conditions: 84.0 versus 84.6 for men, and 81.0 versus 80.7 for women.

However, the regression model shows that this is caused by strongly contingent effects, rather than a lack of effects. The regression analysis was carried out with the same regression model as in the previous analysis, only with expressed party identification used as a predictor, rather than the combined masculinity-femininity score, and with an OLS model, reflecting the wide variation in the dependent variable. While there is no significant main effect of the condition on the participant's combined femininity-masculinity score, there are significant two- and three-way interactions between the predictors. As in the previous analysis, the most

Predictor	Coef	Std Error	z
Condition	−37.69	21.39	−1.76
Party ID	−7.07	2.41	−2.93
Sex	−21.33	8.20	−2.60
Condition × Party ID	8.49	4.13	2.06
Condition × Sex	22.35	13.09	1.71
Party ID × Sex	3.98	1.59	2.50
Condition × Party ID × Sex	−5.00	2.51	−1.99
Constant	119.27	12.02	9.92

TABLE 6: OLS Regression Model for Combined Score.

important effects are bundled into the three-way interaction presented at the end of the regression model. (See Table 6.)

The third analysis makes use of data originally collected by Laurel Westbrook and , Aliya Saperstein through TESS (Time-Sharing Experiments for the Social Sciences) from November 2015 through February 2016, which made use of a representative online sample of US residents. Their module identified 14 transgender respondents among the 2,144 respondents in the overall sample, with another 7 respondents refusing to answer the question. The data used here were generously shared with the authors by Westbrook and Saperstein in 2018.

Another module in the survey (TESS 175) included a 7-point measure of party identification (1 representing Strong Republican, 4 representing Independent/no lean, and 7 representing Strong Democrat, with intermediate categories; mean of 4.1, standard deviation 2.1, 13% Strong Republican, 18% Strong Democrat).

The modules were shuffled randomly, so that half of the individuals (1,072 respondents) received the party identification module before being asked about their current sex and sex at birth, and half (1,072 respondents) were asked about party identification afterward. This latter group was split between those who received the module with transgender items just before the party identification module (556 respondents) and those who had an additional module in between the two other modules (516 respondents).

We made use of logit regression to test three different versions of the expected effect of the transgender items on partisanship responses. In Model 1, the priming variable included only individuals who received the module with the SOGI items just before the module with the party

Predictor	Coef	Std Error	z
Model 1: Only respondents who received SOGI item module just before PID module			
SOGI first	–0.18195	0.0866	–2.1
Model 2: All Respondents who received SOGI item module before PID module			
SOGI first	–0.18126	0.07591	–2.39
Model 3: All respondents who received SOGI item module before PID module, w/Conditional Gender Effects			
SOGI first	–0.19255	0.1068	–1.8
Male	–0.305826	0.10719	–2.85
SOGI first × Male	0.01608	0.15166	0.11

TABLE 7: Party Identification: Ordered Logit Model. Source: Data from TESS.

identification variable. In Model 2, the priming variable included all respondents who received the SOGI items before the party identification question, including those who received an extra module between them. Model 3 included all respondents who received the transgender items before the party identification question. We also examined the expected interaction between sex and the order of the questions. (See Table 7.)

Both versions of the experimental condition variable had significant effects on the respondent's reported party identification, and in the expected direction. In both cases, individuals in the SOGI first condition reported a lower party identification score, indicating a response more toward the Republican side. The very similar effects of the two models imply that it doesn't matter whether the transgender items are right before the partisanship questions or are separated by a few questions.

However, there was no sign of conditional effects by the sex of the respondent (Model 3). That is, it seems that these particular SOGI items made all respondents, male and female, about equally likely to report a more Republican-leaning party identification.

The gun ownership item is taken from the 2018 AP VoteCast survey, a very large survey (139,000 respondents) intended for use as a replacement for traditional exit polling in the 2018 Congressional midterm election. Data from the survey were released to the public in May 2019. Respondents were assigned to one of four question forms, with a small group of respondents receiving all of the items across the question forms, and some items being asked to all of the respondents in a given state, regardless of what question form they were assigned to.

As such, the two LGBT items (described in the chapter text) were asked to 29% of the sample (or about 39,000 respondents), and the gun ownership question was asked to 41,000 respondents (30%). While these items were on separate forms, the gun ownership question was asked to all respondents in two states where gun laws were expected to be an important issue (Colorado and Vermont). Combined with the group that received all of the survey items, this means that 7,488 respondents were asked the sexuality items, and the gun ownership item immediately afterward. As such, the sample sizes for the tables presented are 21,081 (standard deviation of 0.49, which is approximately constant across the categories) for women in the non-LGBT asked group, 12,452 for men in the non-LGBT asked group, 4,516 women in the LGBT asked group, and 2,972 men in the LGBT asked group.

Of those asked the LGBT items, 7% (approximately 2,700 respondents, which is a large sample for these groups) identified as lesbian, gay or bisexual, and a bit less than 1 percent of respondents identified as transgender (0.4% of respondents refused to answer the question). Overall, 45.4% of respondents who were asked the LGBT items said that they had a gun, compared to 42.3% of those who weren't asked.

Because of the enormous sample size of the survey, the margin of error (even for the smaller subset that received the gun ownership and the LGBT items) is miniscule, and the difference between the conditions is significant for both male and female respondents (both differences are significant at $p < 0.01$). However, as we did not hypothesize an effect on female respondents, it is not clear how we should understand it: it could be a display of gender traditionalism, or gender identity, from women. Regardless of the explanation, the difference among women is dwarfed by the difference among male respondents.

The chapter text references comparisons between LGB and non-LGB individuals in the survey. The small number of individuals who identified as transgender (on a separate item in the survey, asked just after the LGB item) were excluded from this analysis, but their inclusion would not impact the results. The sample size for the non-LGB comparison group is small, relative to the overall size of the VoteCast data, because we can compare only those individuals who received the LGB item and the policy question being compared. While there are likely many more non-LGB individuals in the survey, we can identify them only from among those who received the LGB item.

Among Democrats, the only significant difference between LGB and non-LGB respondents is on abortion, where LGB individuals are more supportive of abortion rights, and on views of building a border wall with Mexico, where LGB respondents are slightly less supportive. Interestingly, there are more differences between LGB respondents and non-LGB respondents among political independents, especially with regard to views on Trump, where LGB respondents are much more negative. This may be because respondents who do not have a party affiliation become more likely to rely on other social identities to answer the questions, and an LGB identity is likely more liberal than the identities being relied on by non-LGB respondents. There are not enough Republican LGB respondents in the sample (about 300) to allow for meaningful comparisons. (See Table 8.)

	Non-LGB Democrats		**LGB Democrats**		
Scale	***N***	**Mean**	***N***	**Mean**	**Max of Scale**
Abortion	13347	1.82	1544	1.75	4
Gun policy	2721	1.17	305	1.24	3
Trump favorability	13133	3.74	1519	3.78	4
Support for building a wall	2558	3.40	281	3.59	4
View of immigration	2675	1.17	305	1.13	2
View of ACA	13383	3.36	1541	3.46	4
View of 2017 tax cuts	2442	3.23	272	3.32	4

	Non-LGB Independents		**LGB Independents**		
Scale	***N***	**Mean**	***N***	**Mean**	**Max of Scale**
Abortion	11732	2.19	844	1.82	4
Gun policy	2062	1.50	144	1.32	3
Trump favorability	11240	2.93	799	3.42	4
Support for building a wall	1928	2.74	132	3.38	4
View of immigration	2050	1.37	141	1.23	2
View of ACA	11793	2.60	843	3.10	4
View of 2017 tax cuts	1796	2.67	131	3.11	4

TABLE 8: Issue Positions of LGB and Non-LGB Respondents, by Party.

CHAPTER 5: GOD, GUNS, AND PORNOGRAPHY

Using the public release of the AP VoteCast data (in May 2019), we carried out a logistic regression on whether or not individuals described themselves as "born again" or "evangelical." Among those that gave responses (excluding individuals who refused to respond, didn't know, or were not asked the question owing to the skip pattern), 28% of 43,532 respondents identified as born again or evangelical.

Predictors in the model were a dummy variable of whether the individual was asked the threatening items (29% were); the individual's self-identified political ideology (on a 5-point scale, running from very liberal to very conservative; mean of 2.98, standard deviation of 1.14, 37% moderate, 12% very liberal, 11% very conservative), represented as dummy variables for each point on the scale; the interaction of the threatening questions and ideology variables; and control variables for the form of the survey used. The regression was limited to male respondents, which left a total sample size of 16,399, and a pseudo-R^2 of 0.07.

Results are substantially similar whether or not the form of the surveys is used as a control item, but given that respondents using the different forms completed rather different surveys, the inclusion of the form used as a dummy variable seems appropriate. (See Table 9.)

As is clear from the discussion, the biggest effect of the LGB items was on individuals at the ends of the ideological spectrum, both very liberal and very conservative. The non-linearity in these effects means that it is necessary to represent the data as a series of dummy variables, rather than as a continuous effect, but the sample size is more than large enough to accommodate this. Also note that the form of the survey, as would be expected, has an enormous impact on the results: respondents using the different forms were literally answering different surveys before getting to the items in question. However, the main results persist, with slightly different coefficients, whether we control for the survey form or not.

The data used in the second analysis were collected by a liberal-leaning group, Data For Progress, prior to the November 2018 midterm election, as part of their "What the Hell Happened" initiative. The survey made use of a representative, though non-probability, online sample of registered voters in the United States from YouGov. These data were provided to interested researchers. The overall sample size of the study was 3,215 (unweighted 45% male, 81% white, 38% Democratic without leaners, and 30% Republican). While the data come from an ideological

Predictor	Coef	Std Error	z	P>z
LGB items asked	0.341	0.250	1.37	0.17
Ideology				
Somewhat liberal	0.714	0.298	2.40	0.02
Moderate	0.477	0.253	1.88	0.06
Somewhat conservative	–0.466	0.254	–1.83	0.07
Very conservative	–0.763	0.267	–2.86	0.00
Ideology × LGB items asked				
Somewhat liberal	–0.269	0.310	–0.87	0.39
Moderate	–0.592	0.263	–2.25	0.03
Somewhat conservative	–0.156	0.265	–0.59	0.56
Very conservative	–0.835	0.278	–3.00	0.00
Survey form				
2	–0.559	0.121	–4.61	0.00
3	–0.785	0.121	–6.47	0.00
4	–0.556	0.125	–4.44	0.00
5	–0.268	0.055	–4.88	0.00
Cut point	–1.277	0.2432		

TABLE 9: Identification as Born Again or Evangelical: Logistic Regression.

source, they were collected by reputable sources, and show all signs of being reliable. Note also that the data here come from primary analysis of the complete data files, rather than from any interpretation of the data made by DFP.

Traditional gender views were measured through a three-item hostile sexism scale (Glick and Fiske 1997). Respondents were asked to agree or disagree (on a 5-point scale, ranging from strong agreement to strong disagreement) with the following statements: "Most women interpret innocent remarks or acts as being sexist," "Women are too easily offended," and "Most women fail to appreciate fully all that men do for them." These items were equally weighted and combined into a single 0 to 1 scale, with 0 representing strong disagreement with all of the statements, and

1 representing strong agreement with all of the statements (mean of 0.40, standard deviation of 0.30). As might be expected, men had higher scores on this measure than women (mean of 0.46 versus 0.34), and Republicans (mean of 0.58) had a higher score than Democrats (mean of 0.23). While this scale is generally used to measure hostile sexism, it does so by asking respondents about whether women are pushing too hard, threatening the social status of men (by not appreciating what men do for them or misinterpreting remarks or getting offended too easily). The originators of the scale argue that, "for men, these beliefs reflect the desire to dominate women, see themselves as superior to women, and exploit women as sexual objects—all of which promote hostility toward nontraditional women" (Glick and Fiske 1997). This, of course, corresponds with traditional views of masculinity and gender relations. Views on gun control were measured with an item asking respondents, "Which of the following is closest to your view on gun regulations?" with options on a 5-point scale, ranging from "It should be more difficult to buy all types of guns" to "It should be less difficult to buy all types of guns." Distributional details on this variable are in the chapter text.

The results described in the chapter arise from an ordered logit regression model, in which the dependent variable is response to the gun control item, and the key independent variable of interest is the interaction between gender and score on the sexism scale. Control variables are whether the respondent is unemployed (3.1% of respondents), party identification (on a standard 7-point scale), age (on a 5-point scale, mean of 3.9), education (on a 6-point scale, mean of 4.0), and political ideology (on a 5-point scale, mean of 3.1). (See Table 10.)

The model has an overall sample size of 2,962, with a pseudo-R^2 of 0.18.

In the analysis of firearm background checks, the number of monthly background checks shows significant autoregressive properties of the series at 1 and 2 lags: in plain terms, gun sales tend to be driven by what they were last month and the month before that. There were no significant endogenous factors identified in the state-level data, which are aggregated to the annual level. For the state-level data, the aggregation to the annual level means that seasonality corrections are unnecessary. In the monthly national data, they're included as a series of dummy variables.

The national series shows remarkable growth over time: in 1999, there were about 920,000 background checks per month. Ten years later, in 2009, there were about 1.2 million per month. In 2018, that figure was

	Coef	Std Error	z
Gender	–0.317	0.133	–2.39
Sexism scale	1.699	0.204	8.33
Gender × Sexism scale	–0.530	0.250	–2.12
Unemployed?	0.077	0.202	0.38
Party ID	0.254	0.025	10.04
Age	–0.122	0.033	–3.71
Education	–0.056	0.027	–2.04
Ideology	0.563	0.048	11.77
Cut points			
1	1.503	0.219	
2	3.182	0.228	
3	5.024	0.238	
4	5.567	0.242	
5	7.604	0.280	

TABLE 10: Individual Level Ordered Logit Results on Gun Control Views.
SOURCE: Data from DFP.

2.1 million. Over the whole series, running from December 1998 through October 2018, there were 1.07 million background checks per month at the median (mean of 1.25 million, standard deviation of 596,000).

The model for the number of monthly background checks carried out nationally uses four independent variables: overall unemployment (ranging between 3.5% and 10.6%, mean of 5.8, median of 5.2), men's unemployment (range 3.5% to 12.3%, mean 6, median 5.4), the difference between married men's and married women's unemployment, and the change in the last of those (ranging from –1, indicating a better relative position for men, to 0.9, indicating a worse one; mean and median of 0, a standard deviation of 0.36). The model also includes autoregressive components at 1 and 2. (See Table 11.)

The logic of including all of these indicators jointly is described in the chapter text.

This model has a sample size of 238 (the number of months in the period covered by the data). While standard goodness of fit indicators like R^2 are not available for ARIMA models, the Wald chi-square statistic (84.26 against 6 degrees of freedom, $p < 0.000$) indicates that the model has significant explanatory power.

	Coef	Std Error	z
Change in Married men's minus Married women's unemployment	**201,316**	**42,134**	**4.8**
Married men's minus Married women's unemployment	**–150,323**	**68,211**	**–2.2**
Men's unemployment	120,259	114,389	1.1
Overall unemployment	–107,071	117,738	–0.9
Constant	**–123,081**	**46,026**	**–2.7**
Endogenous effects			
AR(1)	**–0.263**	**0.050**	**–5.3**
AR(2)	**–0.266**	**0.056**	**–4.7**
Sigma	200,850	5,450	36.9

TABLE 11: Effect of Monthly Change in Unemployment Rates on Percentage of Change in Background Checks, National Level.

In general, the state-level analyses are structured similarly to the national analyses described above, but there are some differences. First, due to data limitations, the analysis is on the annual, rather than the monthly, level. This means that we're also excluding the autoregressive and seasonality factors, as they don't apply to annual data. We also exclude the District of Columbia from the analysis: a combination of a small population and strict gun control policies means that very few background checks are carried out (often less than 10 annually), leading to very high volatility on a percentage basis (percentage changes, rather than raw numbers of background checks, are used to allow comparisons between states with wildly divergent numbers of background checks). Finally, as the data consist of 20 measurements of 50 states, it would be disingenuous to count the observations as being truly independent, so we correct the standard errors to account for the 50 state clusters (that is, there are many more data points, but the standard errors are calculated as if there were only 50).

We also present three different models of the relationship, mostly to assuage any concerns about the results being driven by specific modeling specifications, rather than a true underlying relationship. Model 1 does not include the firearms per capita measure, nor its interaction with the economic threat variable of interest. Model 2 adds the main effect of firearms per capita, and Model 3 adds the interaction effect. (See Table 12.)

	Model 1			Model 2			Model 3		
	Coef	Std Error	z	Coef	Std Error	z	Coef	Std Error	z
Change in Married men's minus Married women's unemployment	**0.019**	**0.008**	**2.4**	**0.019**	**0.008**	**2.4**	**0.017**	**0.008**	**20**
× *Firearms per capita*							0	0	2.4
Married men's minus Married women's unemployment	–0.007	0.011	–0.7	–0.008	0.011	–0.8	–0.008	0.011	–0.7
Men's unemployment	–0.016	0.019	–0.8	–0.015	0.019	–0.8	–0.015	0.019	–0.8
Overall unemployment	0.024	0.020	1.2	0.024	0.020	1.2	0.024	0.020	1.2
Firearms per capita				0	0	–1.2	0	0	–1.3
Constant	0.01	0.012	0.8	0.011	0.013	0.9	0.011	0.013	0.9

TABLE 12: Effect of Annual Change in Unemployment Rates on Percentage of Change in Background Checks, State Level.

We limited the time range on the Pornhub trends data to the 2008 to 2018 period. While Google Trends data are available for searches as far back as 2004, and Pornhub has existed as a site since 2007, it wasn't until 2008, at the earliest, that it could be considered a leading provider of online pornography (largely because of bandwidth restrictions in many households before that point). Even so, the Google Trends scores for Pornhub, and all of the categories analyzed, are rather lower early in the period analyzed, requiring us to make use of controls to account for that.

Also note that Google did change the geographic tracking mechanism used to assign individual users to areas in 2011, and changed some aspects of its data collection system in 2016. However, neither of these changes seems to have caused any discontinuity in the data. Some data for after 2018 were also available to us at the time of our analysis, but in some categories and areas, those data were incomplete. To ensure that all the data could be compared, no data from the period after December of 2018 (for the monthly/national series) or after 2018 as a year (for the state series) were used.

As in other regression models presented in this chapter, we have included multiple specifications of the dependent variable and the independent variables, all of which are consistent with our theoretical argument, to show that the results are not driven by any particular specification or set of control variables. In the first set of models (see Table 13), the dependent variable is the Google Trends score for Pornhub for every month in the series (January 2008 through December 2018, inclusive).

In the models presented, we're making use of lagged predictors, in order to better establish causality (as noted in the chapter text). The models vary by the form of the overall unemployment rate used (contemporaneous or lagged change, or both), and the endogenous factors used (moving averages at one month, two months, or both). The idea is to include different combinations, and in the last model presented, all of the possible predictors. Note that the linear time effect (which essentially counts the months in the series) has strong effects throughout the models, reflecting the increasing popularity of Pornhub over the period studied. In all the models presented, the main independent variable of interest (change in relative unemployment among married people) has a fairly consistent effect, with coefficients ranging from about 2.0 to 2.6. While standard goodness of fit measures don't apply to ARIMA models, the equivalent R-squared for these models (based on an OLS regression, absent the

N	130			130			130			130		
DV	**GT Score for Pornhub, Monthly**			**GT Score for Pornhub, Monthly**			**GT Score for Pornhub, Monthly**			**GT Score for Pornhub, Monthly**		
Predictor	**Coef**	**Std Error**	*z*	**Coef**	**Std Error**	*z*	**Coef**	**Std Error**	*z*	**Coef**	**Std Error**	*z*
Overall unemployment rate	2.81	0.78	3.6	3.53	0.88	4.0				1.66	0.89	1.9
Lagged change in overall unemployment rate							–2.54	0.78	–3.2	–1.59	0.82	–1.9
Lagged married men's unemployment rate	–2.94	1.71	–1.7	–1.23	2.33	–0.5	–0.26	2.47	–0.1	–2.73	1.74	–1.6
Lagged men's unemployment rate	3.70	1.39	2.7	2.30	1.80	1.3	4.55	1.93	2.4	4.67	1.58	3.0
Lagged married men's minus women's unemployment rate	–3.95	1.34	–2.9	–5.43	1.35	–4.0	–6.36	1.44	–4.4	–4.28	1.37	–3.1
Lagged change in married men's minus women's unemployment rate	2.03	0.84	2.4	2.37	0.89	2.7	2.57	0.91	2.8	1.97	0.83	2.4
Linear time effect	0.62	0.05	12.5	0.63	0.04	14.6	0.61	0.05	12.1	0.62	0.06	10.2
Constant	–102.84	15.79	–6.5	–106.12	13.70	–7.7	–97.72	15.95	–6.1	–102.43	18.98	–5.4
Endogenous effects												
MA(1)	1.05	0.09	12.4	0.80	0.06	12.8	0.82	0.06	13.5	1.11	0.09	12.6
MA(2)	0.54	0.08	6.8							0.55	0.08	6.6
Sigma	3.02	0.20	14.9	3.59	0.23	15.3	3.72	0.25	15.1	2.96	0.20	15.0

TABLE 13: Effect of National Employment Levels on Google Trends Score for Pornhub, Monthly Data.

endogenous effects) is on the order of 0.90, with much of that driven by the linear time effect.

In the second set of analyses (see Table 14), the dependent variable of interest is the mean Google Trends score for Pornhub within a state. Note that these models do not include endogenous effects, as the annual, rather than monthly, periods of the series renders them mostly irrelevant. The annual periods of the analysis also mean that we used contemporaneous, rather than lagged, effects for the predictors. The year of the data was used in some of the models as a linear time effect. In all the models, the main independent variable of interest is a significant predictor of Pornhub use within the state, with a coefficient similar to that found in the national analyses (despite the dependent variables not being directly comparable). The very high R^2 is the result of the inclusion of the linear time effect, which simply indicates that searches for Pornhub have become more frequent over time.

Finally, we carried out an analysis of the relative popularity of various categories on Pornhub. We did not care to carry out a content analysis of each category, but, thankfully, the evocative category names and clarity of the literature on the topic allowed us to form hypotheses about the categories without that analysis.

To choose the categories to be analyzed, we relied on Pornhub annual reports to identify the top 10 most viewed categories in the United States. To these, we added the categories that were disproportionately popular with women or with men in the United States and were not otherwise included in the top 10. This resulted in a total of 16 categories: lesbian, Japanese, MILF, Ebony, Hentai, Anal, Mature, Threesome, Big Tits, Big Dick, Pussy Licking, Solo Male, Romantic, Hardcore, Rough, and Gangbang. Interestingly, some of the categories that have the clearest relation to the existing literature (Anal, Rough, and Hardcore) are among those that are disproportionately popular with women, rather than men, in the United States. This doesn't mean that they're not popular among men, simply that they're not as popular as the other categories.

We used the same models as for the other analyses, using national-level data taken on a monthly basis. As with the other models, we used multiple specifications, in order to head off any criticisms that the results are dependent on the models used. We will not, however, be presenting the results of all 16 ARIMA regression models, but will summarize the results here.

N	**459**			**459**			**459**		
***R*-Squared**	**0.84**			**0.43**			**0.84**		
DV	**Mean Searches for Pornhub, Annually**			**Mean Searches for Pornhub, Annually**			**Mean Searches for Pornhub, Annually**		
Predictor	**Coef**	**Std Error**	**z**	**Coef**	**Std Error**	**z**	**Coef**	**Std Error**	**z**
Overall unemployment rate	2.42	0.25	9.7	1.25	0.33	3.76	2.67	0.3	8.83
Change in overall unemployment rate				−10.02	2.01	−4.98	−0.91	0.97	−0.95
Change in married men's unemployment rate	−0.95	0.52	−1.8	1.77	1.13	1.57	−0.66	0.58	−1.13
Changed in men's unemployment rate	−1.71	0.36	−4.7	0.10	1.58	0.07	−1.02	0.64	−1.58
Married men's minus married women's unemployment rate				−3.42	0.86	−3.96	−2.10	0.79	−2.66
Change in married men's minus married women's unemployment rate	0.93	0.37	2.6	2.40	0.92	2.6	1.62	0.53	3.07
Year	6.17	0.09	67.5				6.06	0.09	67.42
Constant	−12386.12	184.85	−67.0	39.13	2.12	18.49	−12162.28	181.19	−67.13

TABLE 14: State-Based Models: Regression Results.

MODEL 1

DV: Undifferenced Google Trends result for category

Predictors: Lagged relative married male unemployment, Lagged male unemployment, Lagged married men's unemployment, Lagged Google Trends rank for Pornhub, Linear time effect (month count)

Endogenous Effects: MA 1, AR 1

MODEL 2

DV: Differenced Google Trends result for category

Predictors: Lagged change in relative married male unemployment, Lagged change in male unemployment, Lagged change in married men's unemployment, Lagged change in Google Trends rank for Pornhub, Linear time effect (month count)

Endogenous Effects: MA 1

In both models, the same five dependent variables had significant effects in the expected (positive) direction: Hardcore, Rough, MILF, Ebony, and Anal. Coefficients of the main dependent variable of interest in these models range from about 3 to about 6, depending on the variable and the specification. In neither of the models do any of the other categories have significant effects in either direction. Note that this should not be taken to mean that there is no relationship between married men's relative unemployment and the use of these categories (absence of evidence is not evidence of absence), but simply that there is evidence of such a relationship for the listed categories.

CHAPTER 6: ALTERNATE MASCULINITIES

The qualitative data come from two sources. First, we conducted a content analysis of so-called dad blogs. After a through internet search, we have included all blogs on fathering and parenting in the United States that are run by fathers (corresponding with the other analyses presented in the book). We excluded blogs that had been abandoned or that seemed to function as advertisements. Within the United States, there was substantial regional variation in where these blogs originated. While many blogs are based in New York and California, we also found and included blogs by fathers in other US states, such as Idaho, Michigan, Oregon, and Texas. The blogs were selected based on the description of the blog in the "about" section: we selected blogs that mention being run by dads or being about dads. These blogs address a wide range of topics. While some provide generalized parenting advice, some are more specialized, offering food advice, recipes, fitness advice, video game advice for parents, and children's music. These blogs were read and monitored for one year (July 2018 to July 2019) and were hand coded. The coding was done by the authors and a graduate assistant. The graduate assistant took a class in qualitative research methods and received training at the beginning of the coding process. After the data collection and coding started, the research team had regular meetings to ensure uniformity in coding. Each section was coded by multiple members of the research team to ensure intercoder reliability.

These blogs constitute a public forum that is meant to offer positive messages. In addition to that forum, we have also conducted a systematic, in-depth content analysis of postings to men's support groups. We have made use of public forums including Facebook, Twitter, and Reddit to find narratives from men who have lost their jobs or who are no longer breadwinners for other reasons. Their online groups include a range of men's support groups for stay-at-home fathers and unemployed men. The often socially undesirable nature of the feelings and actions discussed in these posts, especially in the Reddit forums, leads us to believe that these are genuine, rather than strategic, communications, making it reasonable to code them for insights into the internal states of the men posting them. While the posts are public, men using these forums seem to treat them as being private, and often remark on their open and supportive nature, further supporting our notion that they are providing actual insight into the men's thought processes and emotions.

In addition to men's groups, we did a content analysis of postings to forums for women whose husbands have lost their jobs. These women have also formed online support groups to deal with their social and economic changes, and we collected narratives from these support groups. We read and monitored these online forums for one year (July 2018 to July 2019), and these discussions were fully coded and analyzed by two independent coders and compared for inter-coder reliability.

All of these narratives were coded independently by the authors and a research assistant and compared for interrater reliability, with context units consisting of paragraphs covering a single idea, as presented in the text. Cohen's kappa for the coding, weighted by the number of narratives coded, exceeded 0.8.

WORKS CITED

Adjeiwaa-Manu, Nana. 2017. "Unemployment Data by Race and Ethnicity." Fact-sheet. Center for Global Policy Solutions. http://globalpolicysolutions.org/wp-content/uploads/2017/07/Unemployment-Data-by-Race.pdf.

Adler, Alfred. 2002. *The Collected Clinical Works of Alfred Adler*. Bellingham, WA: Alfred Adler Institute.

The American National Election Studies (ANES). ANES 2012 Time Series Study. Ann Arbor, MI: Inter-university Consortium for Political and Social Research [distributor]. Version date May 17, 2016. https://doi.org/10.3886/ICPSR35157.v1.

American Psychological Association. 2009. "The Recession Is Stressing Men More Than Women," *Monitor on Psychology* 40 (7). https://www.apa.org/monitor/2009/07-08/recession.

Arat-Koc, Sedef. 2001. "The Politics of Family and Immigration in the Subordination of Domestic Workers in Canada." In *Family Patterns, Gender Relations*, 2nd ed., edited by Bonnie Fox, 352–374. Toronto: Oxford University Press.

Avina, Claudina, and William O'Donohue. 2002. "Sexual Harassment and PTSD: Is Sexual Harassment Diagnosable Trauma?" *Journal of Traumatic Stress* 15 (1): 69–75.

Banneriji, Himani. 1995. *Thinking Through: Essays on Feminism, Marxism, and Anti-Racism*. Toronto: Women's Press.

Bem, Sandra L. 1981. "Gender Schema Theory: A Cognitive Account of Sex Typing." *Psychological Review* 88 (4): 354–364.

Benach, J., Vives, A., Amable, M., Vanroelen, C., Tarafa, G., and Muntaner, C. 2014. "Precarious Employment: Understanding an Emerging Social Determinant of Health." *Annual Review of Public Health* 35:229–253.

Benokraitis, Nijole V., and Joe R. Feagin. 1995. *Modern Sexism: Blatant, Subtle, and Covert Discrimination*, 2nd ed. New York: Pearson.

Berdahl, Jennifer L. 2007. "The Sexual Harassment of Uppity Women." *Journal of Applied Psychology* 92 (2): 425–437.

Berdahl, Jennifer L., Marianne Cooper, Peter Glick, Robert W. Livingston, and Joan Williams. 2018. "Work as a Masculinity Contest." *Journal of Social Issues* 74 (3): 422–448.

Berdahl, Jennifer L., and Celia Moore. 2006. "Workplace Harassment: Double Jeopardy for Minority Women." *Journal of Applied Psychology* 91 (2): 426–436.

Berrey, Ellen, Robert L. Nelson, and Laura Beth Nielsen. 2017. *Rights on Trial: How Workplace Discrimination Law Perpetuates Inequality*. Chicago: University of Chicago Press.

Besen-Cassino, Yasemin, and Dan Cassino. 2014. "Division of House Chores and the Curious Case of Cooking: The Effects of Earning Inequality on House Chores among Dual-earner Couples." *AG About Gender* 3 (6): 25–53.

Besen, Yasemin, and Michael Kimmel. 2006. "At Sam's Club, No Girls Allowed: The Lived Experience of Sex Discrimination." *Equal Opportunities International* 25 (3): 172–187.

Bittner, Amanda, and Goodyear-Grant, Elizabeth. 2017a. "Digging Deeper into the Gender Gap: Gender Salience as a Moderating Factor in Political Attitudes." *Canadian Journal of Political Science/Revue canadienne de science politique* 50 (2): 559–578.

Bittner, Amanda, and Goodyear-Grant, Elizabeth. 2017b. "Sex Isn't Gender: Reforming Concepts and Measurements in the Study of Public Opinion." *Political Behavior* 39 (4): 1019–1041.

Blau, Francine D., and Lawrence M. Kahn. 2017. "The Gender Wage Gap: Extent, Trends, and Explanations." *Journal of Economic Literature* 55 (3): 789–865.

Bosson, Jennifer K., Jennifer L. Prewitt-Freilino, and Jenel N. Taylor. 2005. "Role Rigidity? A Problem of Identity Misclassification?" *Journal of Personality and Social Psychology* 89 (4): 552–565.

Bridges, Tristan, and C. J. Pascoe. 2018. "On the Elasticity of Gender Hegemony: Why Hybrid Masculinities Fail to Undermine Gender and Sexual Inequality." In *Gender Reckonings: New Social Theory and Research*. Edited by James W. Messerschmidt, Patricia Yancey Martin, Michael A. Messner, and Raewyn Connell, 254–274. New York: New York University Press.

Bruckner, Hannah, and Peter Bearman. 2005. "After the Promise: The STD Consequences of Adolescent Virginity Pledges." *Journal of Adolescent Health* 36 (4): 271–278.

Buchanan, Nicole, and Alayne Ormerod. 2002. "Racialized Sexual Harassment in the Lives of African American Women." *Women & Therapy* 25 (3–4): 107–124.

Bureau of Labor Statistics. 2019. "A-36. Unemployed Persons by Age, Sex, Race, Hispanic or Latino Ethnicity, Marital Status, and Duration of Unemployment." Labor Force Statistics from the Current Population Survey. https://www.bls.gov/web/empsit/cpseea36.htm.

Burgard, Sarah A., Jennie E. Brand, and James S. House. 2009. "Perceived Job Insecurity and Worker Health in the United States." *Social Science & Medicine* 69 (5): 777–785.

Burgard, Sarah A., Lucie Kalousova, and Kristin S. Seefeldt. 2012. "Perceived Job Insecurity and Health: The Michigan Recession and Recovery Study." *Journal of Occupational and Environmental Medicine* 54 (9): 1101–1106.

Burke, Kelsy, and Amy M. Hudec. 2015. "Sexual Encounters and Manhood Acts: Evangelicals, Latter-Day Saints, and Religious Masculinities." *Journal for the Scientific Study of Religion* 54 (2): 330–344.

Butler, Judith. 1988. "Performative Acts and Gender Constitution: An Essay in Phenomenology and Feminist Theory." *Theatre Journal* 40 (4): 519–531.

Carian, Emily, and Tagart Cain Sobotka. 2018. "Playing the Trump Card: Masculinity Threat and the U.S. 2016 Presidential Election." *Socius* 4 (January): 1–6.

Carlson, Daniel L., Amanda J. Miller, Sharon Sassler, and Sarah Hanson. 2016. "The Gendered Division of Housework and Couples' Sexual Relationships: A Reexamination." *Journal of Marriage and Family* 78 (4): 975–995.

Carlson, Jennifer. 2015. "Mourning Mayberry: Guns, Masculinity and the Socioeconomic Decline." *Gender & Society* 29 (3): 386–409.

Carroll, Jason S., Laura M. Padilla-Walker, Larry J. Nelson, Chad D. Olson, Carolyn McNamara Barry, and Stephanie D. Madsen. 2008. "Generation XXX: Pornography Acceptance and Use among Emerging Adults." *Journal of Adolescent Research* 23 (1): 6–30.

Carroll, Joseph. 2005. "Gun Ownership and Use in America." Gallup News, November 22. https://news.gallup.com/poll/20098/gun-ownership-use-america.aspx.

Casler, Krista, Lydia Bickel, and Elizabeth Hackett. 2013. "Separate but Equal? A Comparison of Participants and Data Gathered via Amazon's MTurk, Social Media, and Face-to-Face Behavioral Testing." *Computers in Human Behavior* 29 (6): 2156–2160.

Cassese, Erin C., and Mirya R. Holman. 2019. "Playing the Woman Card: Ambivalent Sexism in the 2016 U.S. Presidential Race." *Political Psychology* 40 (1): 55–74.

Cassino, Dan. 2016. "Why the Upsurge in Gun Sales? Blame Fox News." *Newsweek* June 4, 2016.

Cassino, Dan. 2018. "Emasculation, Conservatism, and the 2016 Election." *Contexts* 17 (1): 48–53.

Catalyst. 2018. "Quick Take: Women in the Workforce—United States." October 14, 2020. https://www.catalyst.org/research/women-in-the-workforce-united-states/.

Chafetz, Janet S. 1997. "Feminist Theory and Sociology: Underutilized Contributions for Mainstream Theory." *Annual Review of Sociology* 23:97–120.

Chamberlain, Lindsey J., Martha Crowley, Daniel Tope, and Randy Hodson. 2008. "Sexual Harassment in Organizational Context." *Work and Occupations* 35 (3): 262–295.

Cheryan, Sapna, Jessica S. Cameron, Zack Katagiri, and Benoît Monin. 2015. "Manning Up: Threatened Men Compensate by Disavowing Feminine Preferences and Embracing Masculine Attributes." *Social Psychology* 46 (4): 218–227.

Civettini, Nicole H., and Jennifer Glass. 2008. "The Impact of Religious Conservatism on Men's Work and Family Involvement." *Gender & Society* 22 (2): 172–193.

Collins, Patricia Hill. 1990. *Black Feminist Thought: Knowledge, Consciousness, and the Politics of Empowerment*. New York: Routledge.

Collins, Patricia Hill. 2000. "Gender, Black Feminism, and Black Political Economy." *Annals of the American Academy of Political and Social Science* 568:41–53.

Connell, R. W. 1987. *Gender and Power: Society, the Person, and Sexual Politics*. Boston: Allen & Unwin.

Connell, R. W., and James W. Messerschmidt. 2005. "Hegemonic Masculinity: Rethinking the Concept." *Gender & Society* 19 (6): 829–859.

Conroy, Meredith. 2015. *Masculinity, Media, and the American Presidency*. New York: Palgrave-Macmillan.

Cortina, Lilia M., and Vicki J. Magley. 2003. "Raising Voice, Risking Retaliation: Events Following Interpersonal Mistreatment in the Workplace." *Journal of Occupational Health Psychology* 8 (4): 247–255.

Cortina, Lilia M., and Vicki J. Magley. 2009. "Patterns and Profiles of Response to Incivility in the Workplace." *Journal of Occupational Health Psychology* 14 (3): 272–288.

De Coster, Stacy, Sarah B. Estes, and Charles W. Mueller. 1999. "Routine Activities and Sexual Harassment in the Workplace." *Work and Occupations* 26 (1): 21–49.

DeMaris, Alfred, Annette Mahoney, and Kenneth I. Pargament. 2011. "Doing the Scut Work of Infant Care: Does Religiousness Encourage Father Involvement?" *Journal of Marriage and Family* 73 (2): 354–368.

Deutsch, Jonathan. 2005. "'Please Pass the Chicken Tits': Rethinking Men and Cooking at an Urban Firehouse." *Food and Foodways* 13 (1–2): 91–114.

Di Tella, Rafael, Robert J. MacCulloch, and Andrew J. Oswald. 2001. "Preferences over Inflation and Unemployment: Evidence from Surveys of Happiness." *American Economic Review* 91 (1): 335–341.

Erickson, David John, and Richard Tewksbury. 2010. "The Gentlemen in the Club: The Typology of Strip Club Patrons." *Journal of Deviant Behavior* 21 (3): 271–293.

Fitzgerald, Louise F. 2017. "Still the Last Great Open Secret: Sexual Harassment as Systemic Trauma." *Journal of Trauma and Dissociation* 18 (4): 483–489.

Foster, Sarah. 2019. "Survey: Nearly 1 in 4 Americans Are Worse off Now Than before the Great Recession." https://www.bankrate.com/personal-finance/smart-money/great-recession-survey-june-2019.

Friborg, Maria K., Jorgen V. Hansen, Per T. Aldrich, Anna P. Folker, Susie Kjær, Maj Britt D. Nielsen, Reiner Rugulies, and Ida E. H. Madsen. 2017. "Workplace Sexual Harassment and Depressive Symptoms: A Cross-sectional Multilevel Analysis Comparing Harassment from Clients or Customers to Harassment from Other Employees amongst 7603 Danish Employees from 1041 Organizations." *BMC Public Health* 17 (1): 675.

Funk, Leahand, and Cherie Werhun. 2011. "'You're Such a Girl!' The Psychological Drain of the Gender-role Harassment of Men." *Sex Roles* 65 (1): 13–22.

Gager, Constance T., and Scott T. Yabiku. 2010. "Who Has the Time? The Relationship Between Household Labor Time and Sexual Frequency." *Journal of Family Issues* 31 (2): 135–163.

Gagnon, John H., & William Simon. (2005). *Social Problems and Social Issues. Sexual Conduct: The Social Sources of Human Sexuality*, 2nd ed. Piscataway, NJ: Aldine Transaction.

Gallagher, Mark. 2004. "What's So Funny about *Iron Chef*?" *Journal of Popular Film and Television* 31 (4): 176–184.

Geiger, Abigail W. 2016. "Sharing Chores a Key to Good Marriage, Say Majority of Married Adults." Pew Research Center, November 30, 2016. https://www.pewresearch.org/fact-tank/2016/11/30/sharing-chores-a-key-to-good-marriage-say-majority-of-married-adults/.

Glauber, Rebecca. 2008. "Race and Gender in Families and at Work: The Fatherhood Wage Premium." *Gender & Society* 22 (1): 8–30.

Glenn, Evelyn Nakano. 2000a. "Citizenship and Inequality: Historical and Global Perspectives." *Social Problems* 47 (1): 1–20.

Glenn, Evelyn Nakano. 2000b. "The Social Construction and Institutionalization of Gender and Race: An Integrative Framework." In *Revisioning Gender*, edited by Myra Marx Ferree, Judith Lorber, and Beth B. Hess, 3–43. Walnut Creek, CA: AltaMira Press.

Glick, Peter, Candice Gangl, Samantha Gibb, Susan Klumpner, and Emily Weinberg. 2007. "Defensive Reactions to Masculinity Threat: More Negative Affect toward Effeminate (but Not Masculine) Gay Men." *Sex Roles* 57 (1–2): 55–59.

Glick, Peter, and Susan Fiske. 1997. "Hostile and Benevolent Sexism: Measuring Ambivalent Sexist Attitudes toward Women." *Psychology of Women Quarterly* 21 (1): 119–135.

Glynn, Sarah Jane. 2016. "Breadwinning Mothers Are Increasingly the U.S. Norm." Center for American Progress, December 19, 2016. https://www

.americanprogress.org/issues/women/reports/2016/12/19/295203/breadwinning-mothers-are-increasingly-the-u-s-norm/.

Goldberg, Abbie E. 2013. "'Doing' and 'Undoing' Gender: The Meaning and Division of Housework in Same-sex Couples." *Journal of Family Theory & Review* 5 (2): 85–104.

Golebiowska, Ewa A. 2019. "Sexual Orientation, Gender Identity, and Political Decision Making." In *Oxford Research Encyclopedia of Politics*. Oxford: Oxford University Press.

González-Val, Rafael, and Miriam Marcén. 2017. "Divorce and the Business Cycle: A Cross-country Analysis." *Review of Economics of the Household* 15 (3): 879–904.

Grazian, David. 2007. "The Girl Hunt: Urban Nightlife and the Performance of Masculinity as a Collective Activity." *Symbolic Interaction* 30 (2): 221–243.

Gutek, Barbara A. 1985. *Sex and the Workplace: The Impact of Sexual Behavior and Harassment on Women, Men, and Organizations*. San Francisco: Jossey-Bass.

Hald, Gert, and Neil Malamuth. 2008. "Self-perceived Effects of Pornography Consumption." *Archives of Sexual Behavior* 37 (4): 614–625.

Harper, Cody, and David C. Hodgins. 2016. "Examining Correlates of Problematic Internet Pornography Use among University Students." *Journal of Behavioral Addiction* 5 (2):179–191.

Hauser, David J., and Norbert Schwarz. 2016. "Attentive Turkers: MTurk Participants Perform Better on Online Attention Checks Than Do Subject Pool Participants." *Behavior Research Methods* 48 (1): 400–407.

Head, Megan L., Luke Holman, Rob Lanfear, Andrew T. Kahn, and Michael D. Jennions. 2015. "The Extent and Consequences of P-Hacking in Science." *PLoS Biology* 13 (3): e1002106.

Heath, Melanie. 2003. "Soft-boiled Masculinity: Renegotiating Gender and Racial Ideologies in the Promise Keepers Movement." *Gender & Society* 17 (3): 423–444.

Hersch, Joni. 2018. "Valuing the Risk of Workplace Sexual Harassment." *Journal of Risk and Uncertainty* 57 (2): 111–131.

Hochschild, Arlie Russell, and Anne Machung. 1989. *The Second Shift: Working Families and the Revolution at Home*. New York: Avon Books.

Hodges, Melissa T., and Michelle Budig. 2010. "Who Gets the Daddy Bonus? Organizational Hegemonic Masculinity and the Impact of Fatherhood on Earnings." *Gender & Society* 24 (6): 717–745.

Hondagneu-Sotelo, Pierrette. 1997. "Working 'without Papers' in the United States: Toward the Integration of Legal Status in Frameworks of Race, Class, and Gender." In *Women and Work: Exploring Race, Ethnicity and Class*, edited by Elizabeth Higginbotham and Mary Romero, 101–125. Thousand Oaks, CA: Sage.

Houle, Jason N., Jeremy Staff, Jeylan Mortimer, Christopher Uggen, and Amy Blackstone. 2011. "The Impact of Sexual Harassment on Depressive Symptoms during the Early Occupational Career." *Society and Mental Health* 1 (2): 89–105.

Hoynes, Hillary, Douglas Miller, and Jessamyn Schaller. 2012. "Who Suffers During Recessions?" NBER Working Paper 17951. https://www.nber.org/papers/w17951.

Huddy, Leonie, and Alexa Bankert. 2017. "Political Partisanship as a Social Identity." In *Oxford Research Encyclopedia of Politics*. Oxford: Oxford University Press.

Issa, Yasmine. 2019. "'A Profoundly Masculine Act': Mass Shootings, Violence against Women, and the Amendment That Could Forge a Path Forward." California Law Review, 107 (2): 673–706.

Kalof, Linda, Kimberly K. Eby, Jennifer L. Matheson, and Rob J. Kroska. 2001. "The Influence of Race and Gender on Student Self-Reports of Sexual Harassment by College Professors." *Gender & Society* 15 (2): 282–302.

Killewald, Alexandra. 2013. "A Reconsideration of the Fatherhood Premium: Marriage, Coresidence, Biology, and Fathers' Wages." *American Sociological Review* 78 (1): 96–116.

Klein, Wendy, Carolina Izquierdo, and Thomas Bradbury. 2013. "The Difference between a Happy Marriage and Miserable One: Chores." *The Atlantic*, March 1, 2013. https://www.theatlantic.com/sexes/archive/2013/03/the-difference-between-a-happy-marriage-and-miserable-one-chores/273615/.

Kornrich, Sabino, Julie Brines, and Katrina Leupp. 2013. "Egalitarianism, Housework and Sexual Frequency in Marriage." *American Sociological Review* 78 (1): 26–50.

Krueger, Alan B. 2017 "Where Have All the Workers Gone?" Brookings Institute, September 7, 2017. https://www.brookings.edu/bpea-articles/where-have-all-the-workers-gone-an-inquiry-into-the-decline-of-the-u-s-labor-force-participation-rate/.

Lee-Won, Roselyn J., Wai Yen Tang, and Mackenzie R. Kibbe. 2017. "When Virtual Muscularity Enhances Physical Endurance: Masculinity Threat and Compensatory Avatar Customization among Young Male Adults." *Cyberpsychology, Behavior, and Social Networking* 20 (1): 10–16.

Livingston, Gretchen, and Kim Parker. 2019. "8 Facts about American Dads." Pew Research Center, June 12, 2019. https://www.pewresearch.org/fact-tank/2019/06/12/fathers-day-facts/.

Maass, Anne, Mara Cadinu, Gaia Guarnieri, and Annalisa Grasselli. 2003. "Sexual Harassment under Social Identity Threat: The Computer Harassment Paradigm." *Journal of Personality and Social Psychology* 85 (5): 853–870.

Magliozzi, Devon, Aliya Saperstein, and Laurel Westbrook. 2016. "Scaling-up: Representing Gender Diversity in Survey Research." *Socius* 2 (1). https://journals.sagepub.com/doi/pdf/10.1177/2378023116664352.

Mansfield, Phillis K., Patricia B. Koch, Julie Henderson, Judith Vicary, Margaret Cohn, and Elaine Young. 1991. "The Job Climate for Women in Traditionally Male Blue-Collar Occupations." *Sex Roles* 25 (1–2): 63–79.

Marsiglio, William. 2016. *Dads, Kids, and Fitness: A Fathers' Guide to Family Health*. New Brunswick, NJ: Rutgers University Press.

McCall, Leslie. 2005. "The Complexity of Intersectionality." *Signs* 30 (3): 1771–1800.

McCann, Carly, Donald Tomaskovic-Devey, and M. V. Lee Badgett. 2018. "Employer's Responses to Sexual Harassment." University of Massachusetts Center for Employment Equity, University of Massachusetts Amherst. https://www.umass.edu/employmentequity/employers-responses-sexual-harassment.

McDermott, Monika L. (2016). *Masculinity, Femininity, and American Political Behavior*. Oxford: Oxford University Press.

McDonald, Paula, and Sara Charlesworth. 2016. "Workplace Sexual Harassment at the Margins." *Work, Employment and Society* 30 (1): 118–134.

McGinley, Ann C. (2016). *Masculinities at Work: Employment Discrimination through a Different Lens*. New York: New York University Press.

McLaughlin, Heather, Christopher Uggen, and Amy Blackstone. 2012. "Sexual Harassment, Workplace Authority, and the Paradox of Power." *American Sociological Review* 77 (4): 625–647.

McLaughlin, Heather, Christopher Uggen, and Amy Blackstone. 2017. "The Economic and Career Effects of Sexual Harassment on Working Women." *Gender & Society* 31 (3): 333–358.

Mechling, Jay. 2005. "Boy Scouts and the Manly Art of Cooking." *Food and Foodways* 13 (1–2): 67–89.

Melzer, Scott. 2012. *Gun Crusaders: The NRA's Culture War*. New York: New York University Press.

Messner, Michael A. 1993. "'Changing Men' and Feminist Politics in the United States." *Theory and Society* 22 (5): 723–737.

Messner, Michael A. 1997. *Politics of Masculinities: Men in Movements*. Lanham, MD: AltaMira Press.

Messner, Michael A., and Nancy M. Solomon. 2007. "Social Justice and Men's Interests: The Case of Title IX." *Journal of Sport & Social Issues* 31 (2):162–178.

Michniewicz, Kenneth S., Joseph A. Vandello, and Jennifer K. Bosson. 2014. "Men's (Mis)Perceptions of the Gender Threatening Consequences of Unemployment." *Sex Roles* 70 (3–4): 88–97.

Miller, Dan J., Kerry Ann McBain, and Peter T. F. Raggatt. 2018. "An Experimental Investigation into Pornography's Effect on Men's Perceptions of the Likelihood of Women Engaging in Porn-like Sex." *Psychology of Popular Media Culture* 8 (4): 365–375.

Morris, Anne. 1996. "Gender and Ethnic Differences in Social Constraints among a Sample of New York Police Officers." *Journal of Occupational Health Psychology* 1 (2): 224–235.

Murrell, Audrey J. 1996. "Sexual Harassment and Women of Color: Issues, Challenges, and Future Directions." In *Sexual Harassment in the Workplace: Perspectives, Frontiers, and Response Strategies*. Edited by Margaret S. Stockdale, 51–66. Thousand Oaks, CA: Sage.

Mushtaq, Mamoona, Safia Sultana, and Ira Imtiaz. 2015. "The Trauma of Sexual Harassment and Its Mental Health Consequences among Nurses." *Journal of the College of Physicians and Surgeons Pakistan* 25 (9): 675–679.

Negra, Diane, and Yvonne Tasker. 2019. "Culinary Entertainment, Creative Labor and the Reterritorialization of White Masculinity." *JCMS: Journal of Cinema and Media Studies* 59 (1): 112–133.

Newton, Judith L. 2005. *From Panthers to Promise Keepers: Rethinking the Men's Movement*. New York: Rowman & Littlefield.

O'Neill, Kevin Lewis. 2007. "Armed Citizens and the Stories They Tell: The National Rifle Association's Achievement of Terror and Masculinity." *Men and Masculinities* 9 (4): 457–475.

Perry, Mark. 2010. *The Great Mancession of 2008–2010*. Statement before the House Ways and Means Committee, Subcommittee on Income Security and Family Support, On "Responsible Fatherhood Programs." https://www.aei.org/wp-content/uploads/2011/10/GreatMancessionTestimony.pdf?x91208.

Pew Research Center. 2007. "Modern Marriage." https://www.pewsocialtrends.org/2007/07/18/modern-marriage/.

Pew Research Center. 2010. *How the Recession Has Changed Life in America*. https://www.pewsocialtrends.org/2010/06/30/how-the-great-recession-has-changed-life-in-america/.

Quinn, Beth A. 2002. "Sexual Harassment and Masculinity: The Power and Meaning of 'Girl Watching.'" *Gender & Society* 16 (3): 386–402.

Roscigno, Vincent J., Steven H. Lopez, and Randy Hodson. 2009. "Supervisory Bullying, Status Inequalities and Organizational Context." *Social Forces* 87 (3): 1561–1589.

Rosin, Hanna. 2012. *The End of Men: And the Rise of Women*. New York: Riverhead Books.

Schanzenbach, Diane Whitmore, Ryan Nunn, Lauren Bauer, and Audrey Breitwiser. 2017. *The Closing of the Jobs Gap: A Decade of Recession and Recovery*. Brookings Institution, The Hamilton Project, August 4, 2017. http://www.hamiltonproject.org/papers/the_closing_of_the_jobs_gap_a_decade_of_recession_and_recovery/?askzja.

Schilt, Kristen. 2006. "Just One of the Guys?: How Transmen Make Gender Visible at Work." *Gender & Society* 20 (4): 465–490.

Schneider, Daniel. 2012. "Gender Deviance and Household Work: The Role of Occupation." *American Journal of Sociology* 117 (4): 1029–1072.

Schneider, Monica C., and Angela L. Bos. 2019. "The Application of Social Role Theory to the Study of Gender in Politics." *Political Psychology* Supplement, *Advances in Political Psychology* 40 (S1): 173–213.

Schultz, Vicki. 2003. "The Sanitized Workplace." *Yale Law Journal* 112 (8): 2061–2119.

Schwalbe, Michael. 2014. *Manhood Acts: Gender and the Practices of Domination.* New York: Routledge.

Silberman, M. S., Tomlinson, B., LaPlante, R., Ross, J., Irani, L., and Zaldivar, A. 2018. "Responsible Research with Crowds: Pay Crowd Workers at Least Minimum Wage." *Communications of the ACM* 61 (3): 39–41.

Simon, William, and John H. Gagnon. 2003. "Sexual Scripts: Origins, Influences and Changes." *Qualitative Sociology* 26 (4): 491–497.

Simonsohn, Uri, Joseph P. Simmons, and Leif D. Nelson. 2015. "Specification Curve: Descriptive and Inferential Statistics on All Reasonable Specifications." SSRN. http://dx.doi.org/10.2139/ssrn.2694998.

Skorska, Malvina N., Gordon Hodson, and Mark R. Hoffarth. 2018. "Experimental Effects of Degrading versus Erotic Pornography Exposure in Men on Reactions toward Women (Objectification, Sexism, Discrimination)." *Canadian Journal of Human Sexuality* 27 (3): 261–276.

Sobal, Jeffery. 2005. "Men, Meat, and Marriage: Models of Masculinity." *Food and Foodways* 13 (1–2): 135–158.

Sojo, Victor E., Robert E. Wood, and Anna Genat. 2015. "Harmful Workplace Experiences and Women's Occupational Well-Being: A Meta-Analysis." *Psychology of Women Quarterly* 40 (1): 10–40.

Stainback, Kevin, Thomas N. Ratliff, and Vincent J. Roscigno. 2011. "The Context of Workplace Sex Discrimination: Sex Composition, Workplace Culture and Relative Power." *Social Forces* 89 (4): 1165–1188.

Stainback, Kevin, and Donald Tomaskovic-Devey. 2012. *Documenting Desegregation: Racial and Gender Segregation in Private Sector Employment since the Civil Rights Act.* New York: Russell Sage Foundation.

Stange, Mary Zeiss, and Carol K. Oyster. 2000. *Gun Women: Firearms and Feminism in Contemporary America.* New York: New York University Press.

Stenner, Karen. 2005. *The Authoritarian Dynamic.* Cambridge, UK: Cambridge University Press.

Stephens-Davidowitz, Seth. 2017. *Everybody Lies: Big Data, New Data, and What the Internet Can Tell Us about Who We Really Are.* New York: Dey Street Books.

Stroud, Angela. 2012. "Good Guys with Guns: Hegemonic Masculinity and Concealed Handguns." *Gender & Society* 26 (2): 216–238.

Sumerau, J. Edwards. 2012. "'That's What a Man Is Supposed to Do:' Compensatory Manhood Acts in an LGBT Christian Church." *Gender & Society* 26 (3): 461–487.

Swanson, Ana. 2017. "The Job Market Just Recovered from the Recession: Men and White People Haven't." *Washington Post*, August 4, 2017. https://www.washingtonpost.com/news/wonk/wp/2017/08/04/the-job-market-just-recovered-from-the-recession-men-and-white-people-havent/?utm_term=.c7df351e20fc.

Takeuchi, Masumi, Kyoko Nomura, Sakie Horie, Hiroko Okinaga, Chithra R. Perumalswami, and Reshma Jagsi. 2018. "Direct and Indirect Harassment Experiences and Burnout among Academic Faculty in Japan." *Tohoku Journal of Experimental Medicine* 245 (1): 37–44.

Tester, Griff. 2008. "An Intersectional Analysis of Sexual Harassment in Housing." *Gender & Society* 22 (3): 349–366.

Texeira, Mary T. 2002. "'Who Protects and Serves Me?': A Case Study of Sexual Harassment of African American Women in One U.S. Law Enforcement Agency." *Gender & Society* 16 (4): 524–545.

Thébaud, Sarah. 2010. "Masculinity, Bargaining, and Breadwinning: Understanding Men's Housework in the Cultural Context of Paid Work." *Gender & Society* 24 (3): 330–354.

Thébaud, Sarah, Sabino Kornrich, and Leah Ruppanner. 2019. "Good Housekeeping, Great Expectations: Gender and Housework Norms." *Gender & Society*, OnlineFirst. https://doi.org/10.1177/0049124119852395.

Townsend, Nicholas. 2002. *The Package Deal: Marriage, Work and Fatherhood in Men's Lives*. Philadelphia, PA: Temple University Press.

Twohig, Michael P., Jessie M. Crosby, and Jared M. Cox. 2009. "Viewing Internet Pornography: For Whom Is It Problematic, How, and Why?" *Sexual Addiction & Compulsivity* 16 (4): 253–266.

Ulrich, Rolf, and Jeff Miller. 2015. "P-Hacking by Post Hoc Selection with Multiple Opportunities: Detectability by Skewness Test?: Comment on Simonsohn, Nelson, and Simmons (2014)." *Journal of Experimental Psychology: General* 144 (6): 1137–1145.

US Department of Labor. 2017. "12 Stats about Working Women." *DOL Blog*, March 6, 2017. https://www.ishn.com/articles/105943-stats-about-working-women.

US Equal Employment Opportunity Commission. Enforcement and Litigation Statistics. Retrieved October 10, 2018. https://www.eeoc.gov/statistics/enforcement-and-litigation-statistics.

Vandello, Joseph A., Jennifer K. Bosson, Dov Cohen, Rochelle M. Burnaford, and Jonathan R. Weaver. 2008. "Precarious Manhood." *Journal of Personality and Social Psychology* 95 (6): 1325–1339.

Weaver, Kevin S., and Theresa K. Vescio. 2015. "The Justification of Social Inequality in Response to Masculinity Threats." *Sex Roles* 72 (11–12): 521–535.

Welsh, Sandy. 1999. "Gender and Sexual Harassment." *Annual Review of Sociology* 25:169–190.

Welsh, Sandy, Jaquie Carr, Barbara MacQuarrie, and Audrey Huntley. 2006. "'I'm Not Thinking of It as Sexual Harassment': Understanding Harassment across Race and Citizenship." *Gender & Society* 20 (1): 87–107.

West, Candace, and Sarah Fenstermaker. 1995. "Doing Difference." *Gender & Society* 19 (1): 8–37.

West, Candace, and Don H. Zimmerman. 1987. "Doing Gender." *Gender & Society* 1 (2): 125–151.

Westbrook, Laurel, and Aliya Saperstein. 2015. "New Categories Are Not Enough: Rethinking the Measurement of Sex and Gender in Social Surveys." *Gender & Society* 29 (4): 534–560.

Wething, Hilary. 2014. "Job Growth in the Great Recession Has Not Been Equal between Men and Women." *Working Economics Blog*. Economic Policy Institute. https://www.epi.org/blog/job-growth-great-recession-equal-men-women/.

Willer, Robb, Christabell L. Rogalin, Bridget Conlon, and Michael T. Wojnowicz. 2013. "Overdoing Gender: A Test of the Masculine Overcompensation Thesis." *American Journal of Sociology* 118 (4): 980–1022.

Williams, Christine L., Patti A. Giuffre, and Kirsten A. Dellinger. 2004. "Research on Gender Stratification in the U.S." In *Social Inequalities in Comparative Perspective*, edited by Fiona Devine and Mary Waters, 214–236. Oxford: Blackwell.

Yoder, Janice D., and Patricia Aniakudo. 1996. "When Pranks Become Harassment: The Case of African American Women Firefighters." *Sex Roles* 35 (5–6): 253–270.

INDEX

INEQUALITIES

A forum for authoritative and innovative social science scholarship on inequality, offering cutting edge research and novel arguments about the most consequential social trend of our time.

David Grusky and Paula England, series editors

—

Michelle Jackson, *Manifesto for a Dream: Inequality, Constraint, and Radical Reform*, 2020

Made in the USA
Monee, IL
06 December 2021